Drama through the Ages

Mary Berry and Michael Clamp

CAMBRIDGE
UNIVERSITY PRESS

CAMBRIDGE UNIVERSITY PRESS
Cambridge, New York, Melbourne, Madrid, Cape Town,
Singapore, São Paulo, Delhi, Tokyo, Mexico City

Cambridge University Press
The Edinburgh Building, Cambridge CB2 8RU, UK

Published in the United States of America by
Cambridge University Press, New York

www.cambridge.org
Information on this title: www.cambridge.org/9780521598750

© Cambridge University Press 1992

This publication is in copyright. Subject to statutory exception
and to the provisions of relevant collective licensing agreements,
no reproduction of any part may take place without the written
permission of Cambridge University Press.

First published 1998
Reprinted 2005

A catalogue record for this publication is available from the British Library

Library of Congress cataloguing in publication data

ISBN 978-0-521-59875-0 Paperback

Cambridge University Press has no responsibility for the persistence or
accuracy of URLs for external or third-party internet websites referred to in
this publication, and does not guarantee that any content on such websites is,
or will remain, accurate or appropriate. Information regarding prices, travel
timetables, and other factual information given in this work is correct at
the time of first printing but Cambridge University Press does not guarantee
the accuracy of such information thereafter.

CONTENTS

INTRODUCTION

This edition of *Drama through the Ages* is one of the Cambridge School Anthologies. This series has been written for students and teachers who want to engage with literature in an active and varied way.

All of the authors included in this book were born before the 20th century began. The collection covers the period from 1400 to 1900. The scripts were written by a range of famous and less well-known writers from Britain, Ireland and France. You may already know the plots of some of the plays and we hope you will enjoy getting to know some new ones.

Wherever possible, the scripts are grouped together by theme or genre so that you can compare how different writers deal with similar ideas or topics. The four sections are in date order, starting from the Middle Ages, so you will get a sense of drama's development through time.

The scripts are printed on the right-hand pages with suggested activities on each left-hand page. You do not have to do all the activities: they are simply a range of possible ways of becoming actively involved in the drama. You can work on some activities on your own or in groups. Many of the instructions – such as suggested group sizes – can be altered to suit your particular needs.

We hope you will find this collection of pre-twentieth-century drama both fascinating and challenging. It is intended as an introduction, to help you discover playwrights, plots and characters that you like and to encourage you to read and perform more of your own choice.

As you read these scripts, you will find many echoes of modern life. People of past times were much like we are today: they enjoyed seeing family arguments, comedies, mysteries, murder stories and interesting reflections of daily life.

We hope you enjoy engaging with and performing these scripts too. Have a good read.

Mary Berry and Alex Madina

MYSTERIES AND MIRACLES
(14th- and 15th-century drama)

The beginnings of drama in Britain

Drama in Britain began in the churches. Services in the Middle Ages were spoken in Latin, which most ordinary people did not really understand. So the priests acted out small scenes from the Bible for the congregation to watch.

After a while, these drama scenes moved outside the churches to the courtyards and streets. Ordinary people took over the acting roles and as they acted out the scenes from the Bible they began to alter them a little. They sometimes added extra scenes to their favourite stories so that they could present interesting characters like the evil King Herod or the Devil. These dramatised stories were called Mystery Plays and became popular in many towns.

The Mystery Play Cycle

In some towns, the organisations or guilds which controlled the medieval trades (like goldsmiths, carpenters, shipwrights, weavers) got together to put on different episodes from the Bible one after the other, in a series or *cycle* of plays. Often a guild would choose an episode linked to their trade, so the shipwrights presented the Noah's Ark story and the shepherds performed the shepherds' story from the Nativity.

A Mystery Play Cycle was performed during the summer on moving carts (called *pageant wagons*). Each wagon would show a different Bible scene. They would assemble about 4.30 in the morning and move through the town, stopping at different points to perform their part of the Bible story. People would stand in the street or look out from their windows to watch each wagon as it came past (see the illustration on page 7).

The most famous Mystery Play Cycles were staged in York, Coventry and Chester. Although the practice of putting on these plays died out many years ago, the York Mystery Plays were revived in the twentieth century and are still performed today.

Street Plays, Miracle Plays, Morality Plays

Acrobats, singers and musicians also performed in the streets in the Middle Ages. There were also Miracle Plays which dramatised the lives of favourite saints, and Morality Plays which told stories of how people are often tempted to do evil. The story of Everyman is the best-known example of a Morality Play.

Performances of the Mystery Plays

A drawing of a Mystery Play being performed in Coventry. The scene on stage shows Noah urging his wife to come into the Ark (see extract on page 9).

Death on the Cross was a common punishment for criminals in Roman times – a slow and agonising way to die. The story of Jesus Christ's crucifixion by the Romans was one of the central scenes dramatised in the Mystery Plays. Part of the script from the York Crucifixion Play is printed on pages 13–15.

Husband and Wife

The story of Noah and his Ark was a favourite topic of the Mystery Plays. In the Bible, God becomes so displeased with all the sinners in the World that he decides to send a Great Flood to drown every living thing. Noah and his family are the only human beings to be allowed to survive. God tells Noah and his family to make an Ark 'of gopher wood' large enough to take his family plus two of every living creature.

Although nothing is said about Noah's wife in the Bible, the tradition arose in medieval Europe of portraying her as a shrew (an aggressive and argumentative woman).

In this extract from the Noah's Flood Mystery Play, Noah's wife refuses to go into the Ark unless she can bring her *gossips* (friends) with her.

"Wife, come in! Why standest thou there?"

1 Quick, before it's too late! (small groups)

Improvise two scenes where one of you refuses to join the others in some activity. One situation could be relatively trivial (such as going to see a particular film), while the other could be much more serious (for example, you are trapped by a fire and have to escape over the roof, but one of you is too scared to move). Then talk about the different ways the group tried to persuade the reluctant one.

2 I'm not going! (groups of six)

Rehearse this extract from Noah's Flood. Think about how Noah and his sons might plead and beg with their wife/mother. Show your play to the rest of the class. Think about how you might create:

- the Ark with its gangplank, the wind, rain and rising floods
- the comedy of dragging the reluctant? drunken? wife into the Ark
- the change of mood in the final moments (lines 38–59)

From the Chester Noah's Flood Mystery Play

[As the flood waters begin to rise, Noah and his family go into the Ark – all except Noah's wife]

NOAH	Wife, come in! Why standest thou there?	
	Thou art ever froward, that dare I swear.	
	Come in, for fear lest that we drown.	
NOAH'S WIFE	Yea, sir, set up your sail,	
	And row forth with evil hail,	5
	I will not out of this town.	
	But I have my gossips every one,	
	One foot further I will not go,	
	If I may save their life.	
	They loved me full well, by Christ;	10
	But thou wilt let them in thy chest,	
	Else row forth, Noah, wither thou list,	
	And get thee a new wife.	
NOAH	Shem, son, lo! Thy mother is wrow:	
	Forsooth such another I do not know.	15
SHEM	Father, I shall fetch her in, I trow,	
	Without any fail.	

[He goes to his mother]

	Mother, my father after thee sent,	
	And bids thee into yonder ship wend.	
NOAH'S WIFE	Son, go again to him and say	20
	I will not come therein today.	
NOAH	Come in, wife, in twenty devils way,	
	Or else stand there without.	
HAM	Shall we all fetch her in?	
NOAH	Yea, sons, in Christ's blessing and mine;	25
	I would you hied you betime,	
	For of this flood I am in doubt.	

---

2 **froward** awkward, perverse	12 **wither thou list** wherever you wish
5 **with evil hail** and may you rot	14 **wrow** angry
7 **But I ... my gossips** unless I have my friends	16 **I trow** I promise
	19 **wend** go
11 **But thou...chest** unless you let them come in the Ark	26 **hied you betime** were quick
	27 **in doubt** terribly afraid

3 Produce a radio play (groups of six to ten)

Rehearse and record a version of Noah and his Wife for broadcasting on the radio. Write an introduction and include sound effects (wind, rain and animals) to make your radio play effective.

'And God told Noah to build an Ark, a huge ship that would hold his family and two of every animal on Earth. And Noah built the Ark just in time, for the rains came down and the floods grew and grew. It was time for Noah and his family to go on board, but when...'.

4 A picture-book Noah for 10-year-olds (in pairs)

Imagine that you have been given the job of creating a picture book aimed at children aged about 10 which tells the medieval story of Noah and his stubborn wife. Include some of the original medieval English words. Here is how you might start.

'God sent down a great flood. Noah knew he had to set sail or drown. All he had to do now was get his wife on board. The problem was that she was a froward awkward lady!'

GOSSIP	[*To Wife*] The flood comes fleeting in full fast,
	On every side it spreads full far;
	Let us drink ere we depart, 30
	For oft-times we have done so;
	For at a draught thou drink'st a quart,
	And so will I ere that I go.
NOAH'S WIFE	Here is a pottle of Malmsey, good and strong;
	It will rejoice both heart and tongue; 35
	Though Noah thinks us never so long,
	Yet we will drink alike.
JAPHET	Mother, we pray you altogether –
	For we are your own children –
	Come into the ship for fear of the weather. 40
NOAH'S WIFE	That will I not, for all your call,
	But I have my gossips all.
SHEM	In faith, mother, yet you shall,
	Whether you will or not.

[*Shem picks her up and carries her aboard*]

NOAH	Welcome, wife, into this boat. 45
NOAH'S WIFE	And have thou that for thy mote!

[*She boxes him on the ear*]

NOAH	Aha! marry, this is hot!
	It is good to be still.
	Ah, children, methinks this boat removes;
	Our tarrying here hugely me grieves. 50
	Over the land the water spreads;
	God do as he will!
	Ah, great God that art so good,
	Now all this world is on a flood,
	As I well see in sight. 55
	This window will I shut anon,
	And into my chamber will I gone,
	Till this water, so great one,
	Be slaked through thy might.

Noah shuts the window of the Ark

28	**fleeting** flowing, pouring	46	**mote** arguing
32	**at a draught** in one go	47	**marry** indeed
34	**pottle of Malmsey** large bottle of sweet wine	49	**removes** begins to move
41	**call** ordering about	55	**well see in sight** can plainly see
42	**But I … all** unless I have all my friends	56	**anon** straightaway
		59	**slaked** stopped, lessened

A Momentous Story

In the York Mystery Plays, the Nailmakers' Guild (would you believe!) was given the job of telling the story of the Crucifixion. In this extract four Roman soldiers prepare to nail and rope Jesus Christ onto the cross.

1 Role on the wall (small groups)

When you perform drama you must have a clear sense of the personality and character of the person you are playing. Read the script opposite aloud and talk about the different personalities of the four soldiers.

Here is an outline drawing of a Roman soldier. Copy it and add a brief description of the character of each soldier. But do not label your descriptions *1st soldier, 2nd soldier....*

Pin each group's character chart on the wall. The class must then decide which soldier is which.

This soldier wants to do the job well . . .

2 A full dramatic presentation (groups of five)

Rehearse a presentation of the crucifixion using the modern English script opposite. Jesus Christ has been ordered to lie on the cross, which is flat on the ground. The soldiers then begin to nail and rope him to the cross before raising it into its final vertical position (see diagrams on page 7). Think about:
- what each soldier does (i.e. who takes what – arm, leg, head and so on).
- giving each soldier a particular character. Who is in charge and orders the others around while avoiding doing any work himself? Who seems to enjoy inflicting pain? Who is unpleasant and not very bright?
- showing the contrast between the down-to-earth soldiers and the suffering of the one they are crucifying. The Bible records that Christ spoke at least some words: 'Father forgive them, for they know not what they do.' Improvise the things that Christ might say – or will your Christ be silent?

Show your version, then talk about how medieval audiences might have reacted to this scene. Would a modern audience react in a similar way?

Modern English Translation of the York Crucifixion Play

(originally written about 1400)

> *Christ is ordered to lie down on the cross.*
> *The soldiers prepare to nail and rope his arms and legs into position*

3RD SOLDIER   We've got to do this job properly.
I think we're just about ready now.

4TH SOLDIER   This villain we've got here,
He's really going to suffer!

1ST SOLDIER   OK then lads, now let's get working.   5

2ND SOLDIER   I think I've got a good hold of this hand.

3RD SOLDIER   I'll pull the other hand right up to this hole we've drilled –
Don't think we'll need ropes to make it reach.

1ST SOLDIER   Well pull, then, and put your backs into it, for Christ's sake!

2ND SOLDIER   Here's a good solid nail – if we drive it through   10
The bone and sinew, it should hold his weight.
No sweat – it's a doddle.

1ST SOLDIER   Hang on a minute, what's going on that side?
Something needs sorting out there.

3RD SOLDIER   This hole's a foot or more out!   15
I reckon his muscles have shrunk.

4TH SOLDIER   No, I reckon the hole's been bored in the wrong place.

2ND SOLDIER   So what? He'll just have to put up with a bit more pain.

3RD SOLDIER   Yeah, the mark was put in the wrong place
That's why the hole is so badly out.   20

1ST SOLDIER   Stop your rabbiting and grab hold of a rope
And pull him from both ends so he reaches the holes.

3RD SOLDIER   Who are you ordering about?
Come and help to pull him into position, damn you!

Now work from the original Middle English script

On the page opposite is the original Middle English version of the script on page 13 where the soldiers go about their business of crucifying Christ.

1 Modern English and Middle English (whole class)

Five students take a part each and read from the modern English version on page 13. The rest of the class follow and read from the original Middle English script.

As each soldier speaks a line from the Modern English script, the rest of the class immediately say together the corresponding line from the Middle English script.

2 Mime and tableau presentation (groups of five)

Choose about 5–6 lines. Present your selection using:
- powerful choric speaking to emphasise the rhyme and alliteration (alliteration is the use of words with the same initial consonant, such as: *Shall **b**ide full **b**itter **b**raid*)
- tableaux (frozen moments which show the action taking place).

3 Radio choric (groups of four or five)

Each group is a different soldier. For example, group (a) is 1st soldier, group (b) is 2nd soldier and so on. Rehearse your lines chorically. Speak together as expressively as you can (perhaps viciously, sympathetically, carelessly, encouragingly). Record your version on tape as if for a radio broadcast.

If you are more ambitious, create an extra group (group (e)) to write a script showing the thoughts of Christ as the soldiers prepare him for death, and rehearse it in the same way.

4 Choices

Choose one of the following:
- Storyboard the events of the script using pictures, modern English and some Middle English.
- Write an account of the Crucifixion as told by one of the soldiers who was 'just doing his job'.
- Write an account as told by a bystander who feels sympathy for Christ's suffering.

The York Crucifixion Play in Middle English

3RD SOLDIER	This forward may not fail;
	Now we are right arrayed.
4TH SOLDIER	This boy here in our bail
	Shall bide full bitter braid.
1ST SOLDIER	Sir knights, say now, work we ought?
2ND SOLDIER	Yes, certes, I hope I hold this hand.
3RD SOLDIER	And to the bore I have it brought
	Full buxomly withouten band.
1ST SOLDIER	Strike on then hard, for Him thee bought.
2ND SOLDIER	Yes, here is a stub will stiffly stand;
	Through bones and sinews it shall be sought.
	This work is well, I will warrant.
1ST SOLDIER	Say, sir, how do we there?
	This bargain may not blin.
3RD SOLDIER	It fails a foot and more;
	The sinews are gone in.
4TH SOLDIER	I hope that mark amiss be bored.
2ND SOLDIER	Then must he bide in bitter bale.
3RD SOLDIER	In faith it was over-scantily scored;
	That makes it foully for to fail.
1ST SOLDIER	Why carp ye so? Fast on a cord,
	And tug him to, by top and tail.
3RD SOLDIER	Yea, thou commandest lightly as a lord;
	Come help to hale him, with ill hail!

Line numbers: 5, 10, 15, 20

---

1 **This forward may not** This job must not

2 **right arrayed** properly equipped

3 **bail** power

4 **bide full bitter braid** feel the pain of our blows

5 **work we ought?** let's get working

6 **certes** certainly

6, 17 **I hope** I think

8 **full buxomly withouten band** very easily with no need for a rope

10 **stub** peg, nail

14 **bargain may not blin** job must be done now

17 **amiss be bored** has been drilled wrongly

18 **bide in bitter bale** suffer a lot of pain

19 **over-scantily scored** marked too short

21 **Fast on a cord** Grab hold of a rope

24 **hale him, with ill hail** pull him, damn you!

HEROES, HEROINES AND VILLAINS
(16th- and early 17th-century drama)

Travelling companies of actors

In the 16th century the trade guilds which had organised the Mystery Plays in medieval times became less powerful. Gradually, groups of actors banded together in companies and travelled from town to town performing their own plays.

The small carts that had been used for the Mystery Plays were no longer large enough, so the acting companies built stages in the courtyards of local inns. This also enabled them to use the doorways, windows and balconies as part of their plays. Ordinary people would pay one penny to stand in the yard to watch. If it rained, both they and the actors got wet. Richer people could pay more money to watch from the comfort of the inn windows and galleries.

The first London theatres

In the second half of the 16th century, the first playhouses were built in London. Modelled partly on the inn courtyard stages and partly on bull- and bear-baiting arenas, they had a central standing area (the pit) with seating galleries all round. The stage extended out into the pit to allow the audience to watch from three sides and get close to the action.

The most famous Elizabethan playhouse was the Globe Theatre where Shakespeare both acted and wrote plays. It was three storeys high and could hold 2,000 people. You can see a drawing of the new reconstructed Globe Theatre on the opposite page.

All kinds of people, both rich and poor, went to the London playhouses. The poorest paid one penny to stand in the yard. Richer people paid two or three pence to sit in the galleries. Sometimes very rich people would pay to sit on the stage itself and annoy the actors by talking during the performance. It would have been a noisy, exciting and sometimes dangerous experience. People sold alcoholic drinks and snacks during the performances and pickpockets, muggers and prostitutes were common. If it rained, the spectators in the open central yard (the *groundlings*) got wet. Once, a spectator's trousers were set on fire during a performance: fortunately his neighbour used a mug of ale to put the fire out. The original Globe Theatre itself burned down when a live cannon, used for sound effects during a performance of Shakespeare's *King Henry VIII*, set fire to the theatre's thatched roof.

Although some of the royal court and the aristocracy enjoyed watching the plays, many Elizabethans looked upon actors as little better than thieves or vagabonds. Women were not allowed to act on the public stage. All the female roles were played by boys.

Shakespeare's Globe Theatre

What Elizabethan and Jacobean audiences loved to see

Most people in the 16th- and early 17th-centuries still believed in the supernatural. They enjoyed plays with witches, ghosts and devils, and stories about human weaknesses, with scenes of murder and revenge. The trapdoor in the floor of the stage would often be used for the entrance of ghosts and devils. Audiences liked to follow the fortunes of great heroes and heroines, cunning and dangerous villains, beautiful and courageous women. They also loved exciting battles and sword fights. One actor was killed during a rehearsal for a fight scene when his opponent's sword pierced his eye and brain.

Christopher Marlowe wrote a very successful play about the legend of Doctor Faustus, who dared to sell his soul to the devil for power, wealth and success. John Webster's play, *The Duchess of Malfi*, is full of dark and evil deeds, madmen, hangmen and murderers. In William Shakespeare's play *Macbeth*, there are murders, witches and a ghost.

The Man who Sold his Soul to the Devil

Doctor Faustus is the story of a man who turns to black magic out of a burning desire
for knowledge and power. Faustus summons up the devil, Mephistophilis, and makes
a bargain with him. In return for 24 years of having whatever he desires – power,
wealth, knowledge, everything – Faustus agrees to give up his soul. This extract is
from the final scene. Faustus's 24 years of power and success are almost up.

1 **Temptation (in threes before you read the play)**

Imagine that a genie appears before one of you. He grants you one wish – but at a
price. The remaining two play the genie. Person (a) is the genie's outwardly
charming, persuasive face. Person (b) is the secretly evil, scheming face – you want
something in return for granting the wish. Show this by speaking your secret
thoughts in asides to the audience. Improvise the following scenes.

- The initial meeting. The person tempted should hesitate at first but eventually
  agree to accept the wish and the payback. Set a date for the payback. The wish is
  made. Finish the scene with a tableau (a frozen picture) which shows how the
  wish comes true.
- Payback time. The genie returns. What does it demand? Finish the scene with a
  tableau showing the emotions of all involved.

Show your improvisation and watch how other groups explored this story. Make a
chart of some of the dilemmas and temptations that you saw.

2 **The questioning circle (large group)**

His time is almost up. Faustus tells his fellow scholars the secret, deadly bargain he
made 24 years ago.

Form a large circle with two of you in the centre as Faustus, and the rest taking the
parts of the three scholars. Read lines 1–49 aloud. Faustus should be full of fear and
despair. The scholars should be surprised, puzzled and concerned for their friend.
- The two playing Faustus should change reader at the end of each sentence.
- The rest share out the three scholars' parts and speak in choral fashion.

3 **In the next room (groups of three or four)**

At line 49 the scholars leave Faustus and go to pray for him in a nearby room. What
do you think they do and say?

Improvise the scene in the next room as the scholars discuss what Faustus has
done, pray for his soul and wonder if the devil will appear.

Doctor Faustus by Christopher Marlowe

Act 5 scene 5

Enter Faustus, with Scholars

FAUSTUS Ah, gentlemen!

1ST SCHOLAR What ails Faustus?

FAUSTUS Ah, my sweet chamber-fellow, had I lived with thee, then had I lived still! But now I die eternally. Look, comes he not? Comes he not?

2ND SCHOLAR What means Faustus? 5

3RD SCHOLAR Belike he is grown into some sickness by being over-solitary.

1ST SCHOLAR If it be so, we'll have physicians to cure him. 'Tis but a surfeit; never fear man.

FAUSTUS A surfeit of deadly sin, that hath damned both body and soul.

2ND SCHOLAR Yet, Faustus, look up to Heaven; remember God's mercies are infinite. 10

FAUSTUS But Faustus' offence can ne'er be pardoned: the serpent that tempted Eve may be saved, but not Faustus. Ah, gentlemen, hear me with patience, and tremble not at my speeches! Oh that I had never seen Wertenberg, never read book! And what wonders I have done all Germany can witness, yea, all the world; for which Faustus hath lost both Germany and the world, yea, Heaven itself, and must remain in Hell for ever, Hell, ah, Hell, for ever! Sweet friends, what shall become of Faustus, being in Hell for ever? 15

3RD SCHOLAR Yet, Faustus, call on God. 20

FAUSTUS On God, whom Faustus hath abjured! On God, whom Faustus hath blasphemed! Ah, my God, I would weep! But the Devil draws in my tears. Oh, he stays my tongue! I would lift up my hands; but see, they hold them, they hold them!

ALL SCHOLARS Who, Faustus? 25

FAUSTUS Lucifer and Mephistophilis. Ah gentlemen, I gave them my soul for my cunning!

ALL SCHOLARS God forbid!

FAUSTUS God forbade it indeed; but Faustus hath done it; for vain pleasure of twenty-four years hath Faustus lost eternal joy and felicity. I writ them a bill with mine own blood: the date is expired; the time will come and he will fetch me. 30

4	**die eternally** am damned for ever	22	**blasphemed** insulted
6	**belike** probably	23	**stays** checks, stops
7	**'tis … a surfeit** he's eaten or drunk too much	26	**Lucifer, Mephistophilis** devils
15	**Wertenberg** University of Wittenberg, in Germany	27	**cunning** knowledge and power
		30	**felicity** happiness
21	**abjured** rejected	30–31	**writ them a bill** signed a deed of sale

4 Faustus's soliloquy as he waits for the devil (whole class)

A soliloquy is a speech where the actor tells his secret thoughts directly to the audience. As midnight approaches, Faustus expresses his desperate wish that Time itself would stop.

Form a circle and read aloud lines 50–61, changing reader at the end of each line. Do this several times.

- Try saying your lines in different ways: sadly, fearfully, urgently, desperately.
- Experiment with one person reading the lines and the whole class echoing words to do with time.

5 From prose to blank verse (in pairs)

Prose is usually the language of ordinary speech. Poetry is often a more intense, rhythmic and emotional kind of language. When Faustus's fear mounts (lines 50–99) his speech moves from prose to a kind of unrhymed poetry called blank verse. This unrhymed verse is made up of five pairs of alternating light and strong stresses (iambic pentameter). Such a rhythm can give a sense of urgency to an actor's speech. Line 54 is a good example:

That time may cease and midnight never come.

Find other lines from this section which have a similarly regular rhythm. Speak the lines to each other so that you can hear the regular rhythm. Now find lines that do not have this regular rhythm and speak them to each other. What is going on in Faustus's mind to cause this change in rhythm? Line 63 may be a good place to start:

See, see, where Christ's blood streams in the firmament!

6 Expressing fear and desperation (small groups)

This chart shows some of the language devices used to convey Faustus's emotions in lines 50–99. Add more examples and decide what emotions they help to express:

Language device used	Examples	Emotions
Repetition (of words and phrases)	*the clock will strike / The Devil will come (lines 60–61)*	*panic or certainty that…*
Exclamations	*ah, my Christ! (line 64)*	*terror*
Questions		
Images (of rising and falling)	*I'll leap up to my God! Who pulls me down? (line 62)*	
Images (of hiding and disappearing)	*Earth, gape! (line 73)*	

1ST SCHOLAR	Why did not Faustus tell us of this before, that divines might have prayed for thee?
FAUSTUS	Oft have I thought to have done so; but the Devil threatened to 35 tear me in pieces if I named God, to fetch both body and soul if I once gave ear to divinity: and now 'tis too late. Gentlemen, away, lest you perish with me.
2ND SCHOLAR	Oh, what shall we do to save Faustus?
FAUSTUS	Talk not of me, but save yourselves and depart. 40
3RD SCHOLAR	God will strengthen me; I will stay with Faustus.
1ST SCHOLAR	Tempt not God, sweet friend; but let us into the next room, and there pray for him.
FAUSTUS	Ay, pray for me, pray for me; and what noise soever ye hear, come not unto me, for nothing can rescue me. 45
2ND SCHOLAR	Pray thou, and we will pray that God may have mercy upon thee.
FAUSTUS	Gentlemen, farewell: if I live till morning, I'll visit you; if not, Faustus is gone to Hell.
ALL SCHOLARS	Faustus, farewell.

Exeunt Scholars. The clock strikes eleven

FAUSTUS	Ah, Faustus, 50
	Now hast thou but one bare hour to live,
	And then thou must be damn'd perpetually!
	Stand still, you ever-moving spheres of Heaven,
	That time may cease, and midnight never come;
	Fair Nature's eye, rise, rise again, and make 55
	Perpetual day; or let this hour be but
	A year, a month, a week, a natural day,
	That Faustus may repent and save his soul!
	O lente, lente currite, noctis equi!
	The stars move still, time runs, the clock will strike, 60
	The Devil will come, and Faustus must be damn'd.
	Oh, I'll leap up to my God! Who pulls me down? –
	See, see, where Christ's blood streams in the firmament!
	One drop would save my soul, half a drop: ah, my Christ!
	Ah, rend not my heart for naming of my Christ! 65
	Yet will I call on him: Oh spare me, Lucifer! –
	Where is it now? 'Tis gone: and see where God

---

33 **divines** religious people
53 **spheres of Heaven** (stars were believed to be supported on huge hollow crystal globes)
59 **lente, lente currite, noctis equi** slowly, slowly run, you horses of the night (Latin)
63 **firmament** heavens
65 **rend not** do not tear apart

7 The movement of a mind (in pairs)

In his last hour on earth, Faustus thinks
about many different things. Draw
pictures which show the range of his
thoughts and fears.
Use a combination of
Marlowe's language
and your own words
and pictures.

8 Create a dramatic climax (groups of six to eight)

Rehearse and present a powerful and frightening performance (or a radio
play) of lines 81–99. Use some of the following ideas:
- Devils echo all Faustus's references to death, Lucifer, Hell and suffering.
- Sound effects: clocks striking, snakes hissing, thunder, sounds made by
  devils.
- Decide how the devils carry Faustus off to Hell. In particular, make line
  99, when Mephistophilis steps forward to claim Faustus, really chilling.

9 The next page in the Victim Log

Imagine Mephistophilis keeps a log to record how he tempts each victim
and how they cope in their final hours. Plan and write
the entry for Faustus. Use your own language and
ideas as well as words from the play script.
Here is one possible format:

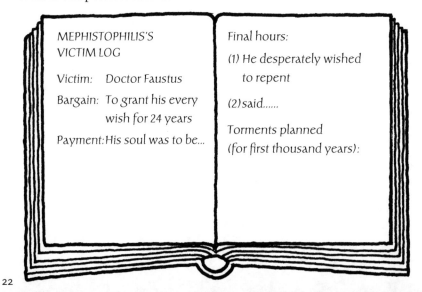

MEPHISTOPHILIS'S
VICTIM LOG

Victim: Doctor Faustus
Bargain: To grant his every
          wish for 24 years
Payment: His soul was to be...

Final hours:
(1) He desperately wished
    to repent
(2) said......

Torments planned
(for first thousand years):

Stretches out his arm and bends his ireful brows!
Mountains and hills, come, come, and fall on me,
And hide me from the heavy wrath of God! 70
No, no!
Then will I headlong run into the earth:
Earth, gape! Oh, no, it will not harbour me!
You stars that reign'd at my nativity,
Whose influence hath allotted death and Hell, 75
Now draw up Faustus, like a foggy mist,
Into the entrails of yon labouring cloud,
That when you vomit forth into the air
My limbs may issue from your smoky mouths,
So that my soul may but ascend to Heaven! 80

The clock strikes the half-hour

Ah, half the hour is past! 'Twill all be past anon.
Oh God,
If thou wilt not have mercy on my soul,
Yet for Christ's sake, whose blood hath ransomed me,
Impose some end to my incessant pain; 85
Let Faustus live in Hell a thousand years,
A hundred thousand, and at last be saved!
Oh, no end is limited to damnéd souls!
Curs'd be the parents that engendered me!
No, Faustus, curse thyself, curse Lucifer 90
That hath deprived thee of the joys of Heaven.

The clock strikes twelve

Oh, it strikes, it strikes! Now, body, turn to air,
Or Lucifer will bear thee quick to Hell!

Thunder and lightning

Oh soul, be changed into little water drops,
And fall into the ocean, ne'er to be found! 95

Enter Devils

My God, my God, look not so fierce on me!
Adders and serpents, let me breathe a while!
Ugly Hell, gape not! Come not Lucifer!
I'll burn my books! – Ah, Mephistophilis!

Exit Devils with Faustus

---

68 **ireful**   angry

70 **wrath**   anger

74 **You stars ... nativity**   You stars whose influence was strongest at my birth

75 **allotted**   given me as my share

77 **entrails ... cloud**   middle of that swelling cloud

81 **anon**   very soon

84 **ransomed me**   redeemed or rescued me

88 **no end is limited**   there is no time limit

89 **engendered**   gave birth to

93 **quick**   alive

99 **my books**   books of magic powers

Shylock – Villain or Victim?

Bassanio needs money to woo and marry the beautiful, wealthy Portia. He asks his merchant friend Antonio for a loan but Antonio's money is all tied up in trading deals. So the two men go to Shylock, the Jewish moneylender. There is one problem: Shylock hates Christians and hates Antonio most of all. All the Christian characters in the play regard Shylock as a villain. How much of a villain do you think he is?

1 Revenge! (groups of three)

Imagine that someone has been bullying another person. The scene may perhaps be in a school or involve an overbearing office manager. Suddenly the bully desperately needs a favour from the victim. Now the victim has the chance to remind the bully of former cruelties and can get some sort of revenge. Devise your improvisation of this scene and show it to the class.

2 Would you trust these Shylocks? (individual or group)

Do these portrayals of Shylock show him as a villain or a victim? Write captions for each picture which make Shylock sound either positive or negative. Read the whole extract and then explain why some of these Shylocks have a knife and scales.

The Merchant of Venice by William Shakespeare (about 1597)

Act 1 scene 3

Enter Bassanio with Shylock the Jew

SHYLOCK	Three thousand ducats, well.	
BASSANIO	Ay, sir, for three months.	
SHYLOCK	For three months, well.	
BASSANIO	For the which, as I told you, Antonio shall be bound.	
SHYLOCK	Antonio shall become bound, well.	5
BASSANIO	May you stead me? Will you pleasure me? Shall I know your answer?	
SHYLOCK	Three thousand ducats for three months, and Antonio bound.	
BASSANIO	Your answer to that?	
SHYLOCK	Antonio is a good man –	
BASSANIO	Have you heard any imputation to the contrary?	10

SHYLOCK Ho no, no, no, no: my meaning in saying he is a good man is to have you understand me that he is sufficient. Yet his means are in supposition: he hath an argosy bound to Tripolis, another to the Indies; I understand moreover upon the Rialto he hath a third at Mexico, a fourth for England, and other ventures he hath squandered abroad. But ships are but boards, sailors but 15 men; there be land rats, and water rats, water thieves and land thieves – I mean pirates – and then there is the peril of waters, winds and rocks. The man is notwithstanding sufficient. Three thousand ducats: I think I may take his bond.

BASSANIO Be assured you may.

SHYLOCK I will be assured I may; and that I may be assured, I will bethink me – may 20 I speak with Antonio?

BASSANIO If it please you to dine with us –

SHYLOCK Yes, to smell pork, to eat of the habitation which your prophet the Nazarite conjured the devil into. I will buy with you, sell with you, talk with you, walk with you, and so following; but I will not eat with you, drink with you, nor 25 pray with you. What news on the Rialto? Who is he comes here?

Enter Antonio

BASSANIO This is Signor Antonio.

SHYLOCK [*Aside*] How like a fawning publican he looks!
I hate him for he is a Christian;
But more, for that in low simplicity   30

1	**ducats** gold coins		14	**Rialto** financial centre of Venice
4	**shall be bound** will have to repay		20	**bethink me** think carefully about this
6	**stead** assist, help		23–24	**pork ... Nazarite ... devil into** to eat pig which
12, 18	**sufficient** financially sound			Jesus conjured devils into from madmen's
12	**in supposition** in doubt			minds
13	**argosy** merchant ship		28	**fawning publican** grovelling taxman
13	**Tripolis** Tripoli		30	**low simplicity** humble foolishness

3 Shylock's opportunity for revenge (two groups of four)

Antonio hates the way moneylenders like Shylock charge interest and has cruelly insulted him in the past. Now he is forced to go to Shylock for a loan. The Jew has good reason to hate this Christian.

The picture below shows how these three men may seem very polite on the outside, but are secretly far from friendly. Rehearse and present lines 1–53 to the rest of the class in these two ways:

Group a: Three of you speak Antonio, Bassanio and Shylock's lines. The fourth is Shylock's *alter ego* (a voice expressing his hidden thoughts). The alter ego should cut in on the dialogue at suitable moments. When you write your script for Shylock's alter ego you should consider:
- why Shylock deliberately makes Bassanio wait for an answer (lines 1–18)
- why he mentions pirates and other perils of the sea (lines 11–18)
- his reasons for hating Antonio (lines 28–38)
- whether he really forgets the terms of the agreement (lines 45–54)
- what he is thinking as he greets Antonio (lines 46–47).

Group b: Three of you speak Antonio, Bassanio and Shylock's lines. The fourth person is Antonio's *alter ego* cutting in on the dialogue at suitable moments. When scripting Antonio's *alter ego* consider:
- why Antonio sent Bassanio ahead to talk to Shylock about the loan
- what Antonio is thinking while Shylock speaks his long aside (lines 28–39)
- how confident Antonio is that he can pay back the loan (lines 11–18).

ANTONIO
Alter ego: 'I hate this Jew but I need his money.'

SHYLOCK
'Antonio is a good man'
Alter ego: 'And may he rot in hell.'

He lends out money gratis, and brings down
The rate of usance here with us in Venice.
If I can catch him once upon the hip,
I will feed fat the ancient grudge I bear him.
He hates our sacred nation, and he rails   35
Even there where merchants most do congregate
On me, my bargains, and my well-won thrift
Which he calls interest. Cursed be my tribe
If I forgive him!

BASSANIO   Shylock, do you hear?

SHYLOCK I am debating of my present store,   40
And by the near guess of my memory
I cannot instantly raise up the gross
Of full three thousand ducats. What of that?
Tubal, a wealthy Hebrew of my tribe,
Will furnish me. But soft, how many months   45
Do you desire? [*To Antonio*] Rest you fair, good signor!
Your worship was the last man in our mouths.

ANTONIO Shylock, albeit I neither lend nor borrow
By taking nor by giving of excess,
Yet to supply the ripe wants of my friend   50
I'll break a custom. [*To Bassanio*] Is he yet possessed
How much ye would?

SHYLOCK   Ay, ay, three thousand ducats.

ANTONIO And for three months.

SHYLOCK I had forgot, three months; [*To Bassanio*] you told me so.
Well then, your bond; and let me see – but hear you,   55
Methought you said you neither lend nor borrow
Upon advantage.

ANTONIO   I do never use it.

SHYLOCK When Jacob grazed his uncle Laban's sheep –
This Jacob from our holy Abram was –
ANTONIO And what of him, did he take interest?   60

---

31 **gratis** without charging interest
32 **rate of usance** rate of interest
33 **upon the hip** in a weak spot
35 **rails** criticises
37 **thrift** profit
40 **I am … store** I'm working out how much ready cash I have

42 **gross** full amount
47 **in our mouths** we were talking about
48 **albeit … excess** although I don't lend or borrow for profit
50 **ripe wants** urgent needs
59 **Abram** Abraham (ancient Jewish leader)

4 Let me tell you a story (groups of three)

Shylock knows Antonio hates moneylending, but now he has the chance to justify his method of charging interest on loans. He tells how, in the Bible, Jacob made a profit from his uncle's sheep.

Jacob agreed to look after his uncle Laban's sheep on condition that he could keep any 'eanlings' (new-born lambs) that were 'streaked and pied' (multicoloured). When the ewes were 'rank' (ready to mate), Jacob 'pilled me certain wands' (peeled the bark off some branches to create a striped effect) and made a fence of them. People believed in those days that what a mother saw during conception affected her offspring. When the lambs were born, many of them were streaked and pied, so Jacob was able to keep them for himself.

- Take it in turns to tell Shylock's story (lines 61–75). Antonio and Bassanio decide how to behave while listening to Shylock.
- Draw a series of pictures/cartoons comparing how Jacob gets himself a large number of new-born lambs with how Shylock gets himself large sums of money. Here is an idea of how you might start:

The skilful shepherd peeled some branches and 'stuck them up before the fulsome ewes'.

Shylock lends money out 'upon advantage' believing he will make money doing so.

SHYLOCK No, not take interest, not as you would say
Directly interest. Mark what Jacob did:
When Laban and himself were compromised
That all the eanlings which were streaked and pied
Should fall as Jacob's hire, the ewes being rank   65
In end of autumn turnèd to the rams,
And when the work of generation was
Between these woolly breeders in the act,
The skilful shepherd pilled me certain wands
And in the doing of the deed of kind   70
He stuck them up before the fulsome ewes,
Who then conceiving, did in eaning time
Fall parti-coloured lambs, and those were Jacob's.
This was a way to thrive, and he was blest;
And thrift is blessing if men steal it not.   75

ANTONIO This was a venture, sir, that Jacob served for,
A thing not in his power to bring to pass,
But swayed and fashioned by the hand of heaven.
Was this inserted to make interest good?
Or is your gold and silver ewes and rams?   80

SHYLOCK I cannot tell, I make it breed as fast.
But note me, signor –

ANTONIO   Mark you this, Bassanio,
The devil can cite Scripture for his purpose.
An evil soul producing holy witness
Is like a villain with a smiling cheek,   85
A goodly apple rotten at the heart.
O what a goodly outside falsehood hath!

SHYLOCK Three thousand ducats, 'tis a good round sum.
Three months from twelve, then let me see, the rate –

ANTONIO Well, Shylock, shall we be beholding to you?   90

63	**compromised** agreed	71	**fulsome** on heat, ready for mating
64	**eanlings** new-born lambs	72	**eaning time** lambing time
64	**streaked and pied** multicoloured	73	**parti-coloured** multicoloured
65	**hire** wages	76–78	**This was ... heaven** God was responsible for
65	**rank** ready to mate		Jacob's good fortune
67	**work of generation** mating	79	**inserted** mentioned
69	**pilled ... wands** peeled the bark from some	84	**holy witness** evidence from the Bible
	branches to create a striped effect	89	**the rate** interest charge
70	**deed of kind** act of mating	90	**beholding** indebted

5 Shylock gives vent to his anger (groups of about six)

Two of you take the parts of Antonio and Bassanio. The rest divide up lines 91–114 between you and create a 'group Shylock'. Try different ways of showing your resentment of the two Christians:

- perhaps you circle round Antonio in a very aggressive and sneering manner
- perhaps you sit back in your chairs, mocking and laughing cruelly.

Speak the lines chorically, or use a choric echo to emphasise particular phrases like 'cut-throat dog'.

6 Show the scene at the Rialto (individual or small groups)

Shylock tells us in detail how Antonio used to treat him when they met at the Rialto Bridge (lines 91–114). This bridge was where the merchants and financiers of Venice gathered to do business.

Read what Shylock says and imagine what some of these meetings might have felt like.

Draw two or three illustrations of these meetings, with captions, like the one on the right. Underneath write an account of the meeting that Shylock might have written in his diary.

'You that did void your rheum upon my beard'

SHYLOCK   Signor Antonio, many a time and oft
In the Rialto you have rated me
About my monies and my usances.
Still have I borne it with a patient shrug
For suff'rance is the badge of all our tribe.   95
You call me misbeliever, cut-throat dog,
And spit upon my Jewish gaberdine,
And all for use of that which is mine own.
Well then, it now appears you need my help.
Go to, then, you come to me, and you say,   100
'Shylock, we would have monies' – you say so,
You that did void your rheum upon my beard,
And foot me as you spurn a stranger cur
Over your threshold: monies is your suit.
What should I say to you? Should I not say   105
'Hath a dog money? Is it possible
A cur can lend three thousand ducats?' Or
Shall I bend low, and in a bondman's key,
With bated breath and whispering humbleness,
Say this: 110
'Fair sir, you spat on me on Wednesday last,
You spurned me such a day, another time
You called me dog: and for these courtesies
I'll lend you thus much monies.'
ANTONIO   I am as like to call thee so again,   115
To spit on thee again, to spurn thee too.
If thou wilt lend this money, lend it not
As to thy friends, for when did friendship take
A breed for barren metal of his friend?
But lend it rather to thine enemy,   120
Who if he break, thou mayst with better face
Exact the penalty.
SHYLOCK   Why look you how you storm!
I would be friends with you, and have your love,
Forget the shames that you have stained me with,   125
Supply your present wants, and take no doit
Of usance for my monies, and you'll not hear me.
This is kind I offer.
BASSANIO   This were kindness.

92	**rated** insulted	108	**a bondman's key** the
93	**usances** charging of interest		voice of a slave
95	**suff'rance** enduring suffering	118–19	**take a breed ... of his friend?**
97	**gaberdine** coat		charge a fee for lending
102	**void your rheum** spit		money to his friend?
103	**stranger cur** stray dog		

126–27	**take no doit of usance**
	charge you no interest at all

7 'I would be friends with you' (groups of three)

Shylock makes an offer of friendship (lines 124–37). He will charge Antonio no interest ('no doit of usance') for the loan of the 3,000 ducats. If Antonio fails to repay the loan on the appointed day, all Shylock will demand is a pound of flesh from Antonio's body.

Take a part each and read lines 129–67. Then write notes on the following topics:

- Antonio's reaction: does he believe Shylock's offer of friendship? Find quotations to support your view.
- Bassanio's reaction: does he believe Shylock means Antonio no harm? Find quotations to support your view.
- Would you would trust Shylock? Write what he might be secretly thinking as he speaks with Antonio and Bassanio.

8 Is Shylock a villain? (in pairs)

Many Elizabethans distrusted Jewish people. As a group they had been officially banned from England since the early 14th century. Some, however, were unofficially allowed to stay, but they were never permitted to become a part of English life and were barred from taking up many trades. This is why some of them (like Shylock) took to moneylending, which many Elizabethans (like Antonio) regarded as an unchristian practice. Attacks on Jewish communities in England have occurred through the centuries. One such anti-Jewish riot in York in 1190 led to the death of 150 Jews.

In the dictionary a *villain* is a deeply wicked man. How villainous do you think Shylock is? Collect your ideas and evidence onto a chart like the one below:

	Evidence that Shylock is a villain	Evidence that Shylock is a victim
The way Shylock behaves	*how he smiles and appears friendly, but we know…*	*'I have born it with a patient shrug': this shows…*
The language Shylock uses (especially insincere language)	*He tells us secretly 'I hate (Antonio) for he is a Christian' but says to Antonio 'Rest you fair, good signor!'*	
The way other characters behave towards him		*Antonio spits on him: 'I am as like to call thee so again, to spit on thee again'*
The way other characters speak about him	*'a villain with a smiling cheek'*	

Use the evidence collected in your chart to plan and write an essay: Is Shylock a villain or a victim?

SHYLOCK	This kindness will I show.	130
	Go with me to a notary, seal me there	
	Your single bond, and, in a merry sport,	
	If you repay me not on such a day,	
	In such a place, such sum or sums as are	
	Expressed in the condition, let the forfeit	135
	Be nominated for an equal pound	
	Of your fair flesh, to be cut off and taken	
	In what part of your body pleaseth me.	
ANTONIO	Content, in faith! I'll seal to such a bond,	
	And say there is much kindness in the Jew.	140
BASSANIO	You shall not seal to such a bond for me.	
ANTONIO	Why, fear not, man, I will not forfeit it.	
	Within these two months, that's a month before	
	This bond expires, I do expect return	
	Of thrice three times the value of this bond.	145
SHYLOCK	O father Abram, what these Christians are,	
	Whose own hard dealings teaches them suspect	
	The thoughts of others! Pray you tell me this:	
	If he should break his day what should I gain	
	By the exaction of the forfeiture?	150
	A pound of man's flesh, taken from a man,	
	Is not so estimable, profitable neither,	
	As flesh of muttons, beefs, or goats. I say	
	To buy his favour, I extend this friendship.	
	If he will take it, so; if not, adieu,	155
	And for my love, I pray you wrong me not.	
ANTONIO	Yes, Shylock, I will seal unto this bond.	
SHYLOCK	Then meet me forthwith at the notary's.	
	Give him direction for this merry bond,	
	And I will go and purse the ducats straight,	160
	See to my house left in the fearful guard	
	Of an unthrifty knave, and presently	
	I'll be with you. [*Exit Shylock*]	
ANTONIO	Hie thee, gentle Jew.	
	The Hebrew will turn Christian, he grows kind.	
BASSANIO	I like not fair terms and a villain's mind.	165
ANTONIO	Come on, in this there can be no dismay,	
	My ships come home a month before the day.	

---

131 **notary** lawyer
132 **single bond** an agreement with no conditions made on it
132 **in a merry sport** just for a joke

150 **exaction of the forfeiture** claiming the penalty (of a pound of flesh)
152 **estimable** valuable

162 **unthrifty knave** careless servant
162 **presently** straight away
163 **Hie thee, gentle Jew** Off you go, noble Jew

Brother and Sister: Villain and Heroine

The Duchess of Malfi, a widow, has secretly re-married. Her brothers are enraged, because they will not now inherit her lands and title. One brother, Ferdinand, captures the Duchess and her children. He plans to have them all killed, but not before he has tormented the Duchess cruelly. First, he sends a group of madmen from the nearby asylum to sing and dance for her 'entertainment'.

1 Ferdinand orders the death of the Duchess (in pairs)

Read the extract through. Note everything Bosola, the hired killer, does and how he behaves towards the Duchess. Use these notes to improvise an earlier scene where Ferdinand and Bosola plan the Duchess's murder.

2 A moment with the madmen (groups of six to eight)

The madmen have been sent by Ferdinand to torture the Duchess with their manic behaviour and weird dancing. Create a *tableau* (a frozen picture) of a moment during the dance.

3 'I am come to make thy tomb' (groups of about eight)

Take parts as the Duchess, Bosola, Servant, Madmen and rehearse lines 1–27. Concentrate on creating the noise and crazy movement of the madmen, followed by the sudden change in atmosphere as Bosola enters. Think about the following:
- Is the Duchess frightened by the madmen?
- Is the servant afraid, or reluctant to leave? How much does he know?
- Is the Duchess's reply to Bosola's menacing words calm, scared, or defiant?

The Duchess of Malfi by John Webster (about 1613)

Act 4 scene 2

The eight madmen start to dance to the sound of manic music. Then Bosola, the hired killer, enters. He is disguised as an old man

DUCHESS Is he mad too?

SERVANT   Pray, question him; I'll leave you.

Exit Servant and Madmen

BOSOLA I am come to make thy tomb.

DUCHESS   Ha! my tomb?
Thou speakst as if I lay upon my death-bed,
Gasping for breath: dost thou perceive me sick?

BOSOLA Yes, and the more dangerously, since thy sickness is insensible.   **5**

DUCHESS Thou art not mad, sure: dost know me?

BOSOLA Yes.

DUCHESS Who am I?

BOSOLA Thou art a box of worm seed. What's this flesh? A little crudded milk,
fantastical puff paste. Our bodies are weaker than those paper prisons   **10**
boys use to keep flies in: more contemptible, since ours is to preserve earth-
worms: didst thou ever see a lark in a cage? Such is the soul in the body.

DUCHESS Am not I thy Duchess?

BOSOLA Thou art some great woman, sure; for riot begins to sit on thy forehead (clad in
grey hairs) twenty years sooner than on a merry milkmaid's. Thou sleepest   **15**
worse, than if a mouse should be forced to take up her lodging in a cat's ear.

DUCHESS I am Duchess of Malfi still.

BOSOLA That makes thy sleeps so broken:
Glories, like glow-worms, afar off shine bright,
But looked to near, have neither heat nor light.   **20**

DUCHESS Thou art very plain.

BOSOLA My trade is to flatter the dead, not the living; I am a tomb maker.

DUCHESS And thou comest to make my tomb?

BOSOLA Yes.

DUCHESS Let me know fully therefore the effect   **25**
Of this thy dismal preparation,
This talk, fit for a charnel.

BOSOLA   Now I shall;

Enter Executioners with a coffin, cords and a bell

---

5 **is insensible** cannot be seen

9 **box of worm seed** potential breeding ground for worms

9 **crudded** curdled

10 **puff paste** light, insubstantial pastry

14 **riot** disorder, disintegration, decay

19 **Glories** worldly fame and position

21 **plain** blunt, to the point

27 **charnel** burial vault

4 Fill the Duchess with terror (whole class)

Bosola plans to torment the Duchess before he kills her. Present lines 27–51 as a whole class drama. Begin with the entrance of the Executioners.

- Several of you act as the Executioners carrying coffin, rope and bell. Be menacing and cruel. Begin with the entrance of the Executioners.
- Three of you play the roles of the Duchess, Bosola and Cariola. Bosola says he is Death ('the common bellman'). How should he behave? Decide which woman is most frightened.
- The rest of the class form a large circle around the players to say lines 38–47. Experiment with different ways of speaking: chanting, whispering ... Bosola repeats line 47 after you.

5 Write your own dirge (in pairs)

If you speak Bosola's funeral dirge or death-song (lines 38–47), you will notice that the verse has a rhythmic beat:

```
    /   ∪  /  ∪ /  ∪ /
```
Hark now everything is still

```
  ∪    /   /  ∪ ∪  / ∪  /
```
The screech-owl and the whistler shrill

Write your own dirge. Start by drawing and describing ideas and images connected with death and darkness:

  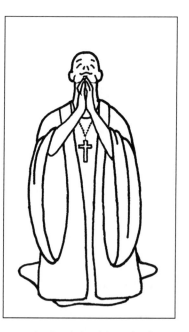

How Nature responds to death: *dog howls, stars go out, wind blows*

How Death looks: *figure in black, with scythe, face of a skull*

How the dying should prepare for death: *say prayers, put on suitable clothes, make farewells*

> Here is a present from your princely brothers,
> And may it arrive welcome, for it brings
> Last benefit, last sorrow.

DUCHESS   Let me see it.   30

BOSOLA   This is your last presence chamber.

CARIOLA O my sweet lady!

DUCHESS   Peace; it affrights not me.

BOSOLA   I am the common bellman,
> That usually is sent to condemned persons,
> The night before they suffer.

DUCHESS   Even now thou saidst   35
> Thou wast a tomb-maker?

BOSOLA   It was to bring you
> By degrees to mortification. Listen:

He rings the bell, Executioners approach

> Hark, now everything is still,
> The screech-owl and the whistler shrill
> Call upon our Dame, aloud,   40
> And bid her quickly don her shroud!
> Strew your hair with powders sweet,
> Don clean linen, bathe your feet,
> And, the foul fiend more to check,
> A crucifix let bless your neck.   45
> 'Tis now full tide 'tween night and day,
> End your groan, and come away.

Executioners approach

CARIOLA Hence villains, tyrants, murderers! Alas! What will you do with my
> lady? Call for help.

DUCHESS To whom? To our next neighbours? They are mad-folks.   50

BOSOLA   Remove that noise.

Executioners seize Cariola, who struggles

DUCHESS   Farewell Cariola.

CARIOLA   I will die with her.

DUCHESS I pray thee look thou givest my little boy
> Some syrup for his cold, and let the girl
> Say her prayers, ere she sleep.

Cariola is forced off

---

31 **last presence chamber** final reception room to receive your guests

33 **bellman** watchman who rings bell before executions and burials

37 **mortification** being ready for death

39 **whistler** bird with harsh cry

41 **shroud** burial sheet

52 **look thou givest** make sure you give

6 Show the death of the Duchess (groups of about four)

Despite all Bosola's efforts, the Duchess meets her death without fear. Two of you take the parts of Bosola and Duchess, the others are the Executioners. Read from line 54 (*Cariola is forced off*) to line 79 (*they strangle the Duchess*).

Select key phrases from this section and use them to write a short script, with stage directions (use some of your own words if you wish). Here is how your script might begin:

DUCHESS	*[turns to Bosola] What death?*
BOSOLA	*Strangling. Here are your executioners.*
DUCHESS	*I forgive them.*
BOSOLA	*Does not death frighten you?*
DUCHESS	*What is there to be afraid of?*
BOSOLA	*But this rope should terrify you [shows her the noose].*

Memorise your script and present your version of the Duchess's death to the rest of the class. Finish with a tableau.

7 Three reasons to live (groups of four)

Cariola will beg for mercy before she is killed. Before you look at how she dies, try the following improvisation. Imagine that two murderers enter the room. Their orders are to kill the two prisoners who wait there.

- **Pair a**: You are the victims. You must prepare as many excuses as you can to delay your death.
- **Pair b**: You are the merciless killers. Whatever excuse is given, you argue against it, unless you meet with an excuse you cannot oppose, in which case you must release your prisoners.

Improvise the scene. Then read how Cariola tries to save herself (lines 83–94). What reasons does Cariola think of to persuade Bosola to let her live and what answers does he give?

8 Irony (individual or groups)

Cariola's wish to be killed with the Duchess ('I will die with her': line 51) is granted, but in a grimly ironic way. *Irony* is when a character in a play says something which seems to have one meaning but turns out later to have a rather different meaning. Cariola is not actually killed with her mistress but she does in one sense 'die with her'. Can you explain how?

	Now what you please,	
	What death?	55
BOSOLA	Strangling. Here are your executioners.	
DUCHESS	I forgive them.	
BOSOLA	Doth not death frighten you?	
DUCHESS	Who would be afraid of it?	

Knowing to meet such excellent company
In the other world.

BOSOLA Yet, methinks, 60
The manner of your death should much afflict you,
This cord should terrify you?

DUCHESS Not a whit:
What would it pleasure me, to have my throat cut
With diamonds? Or to be smothered
With cassia? Or to be shot to death, with pearls? 65
I know death hath ten thousand several doors
For men to take their Exits. Tell my brothers
That I perceive death, now I am well awake,
Best gift is, they can give, or I can take.
I would fain put off my last woman's fault,
I'd not be tedious to you. 70

EXECUTIONERS We are ready.

DUCHESS Dispose my breath how please you, but my body
Bestow upon my women, will you?

EXECUTIONERS Yes.

DUCHESS Pull, and pull strongly, for your able strength
Must pull down heaven upon me. 75
Yet stay, heaven gates are not so highly arched
As princes' palaces: they that enter there
Must go upon their knees [*kneels*]. Come violent death,
Serve for mandragora to make me sleep!

The Executioners strangle the Duchess

BOSOLA Where's the waiting woman?
Fetch her. Some other strangle the children. 80

Exit Executioners. They re-enter with Cariola

Look you, there sleeps your mistress.

---

61 much afflict you really
frighten you

62 not a whit not in the least

65 cassia a fragrant spice

66 several separate, different

69 fain gladly

79 mandragora narcotic drug
made from a mandrake root

9 Compare the Duchess and Cariola (groups of about 5)

Read aloud lines 48–94 (from the entrance of the Executioners to the strangling of Cariola). The Duchess and Cariola face up to death in very different ways. Compare the way the two women speak and behave. Record your thoughts on spider diagrams like these:

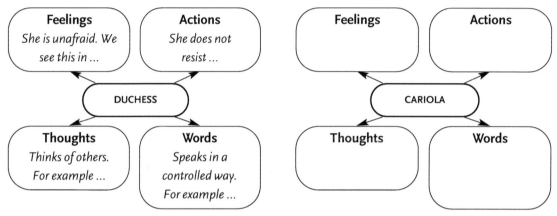

Feelings
She is unafraid. We see this in …

Actions
She does not resist …

DUCHESS

Thoughts
Thinks of others. For example …

Words
Speaks in a controlled way. For example …

Feelings

Actions

CARIOLA

Thoughts

Words

10 'Cover her face. Mine eyes dazzle. She died young' (in pairs)

Ferdinand, the Duchess's brother, enters to inspect the bodies (line 94). Read lines 94–105 and then choose *one* of the following activities.

Dramatisation: Cut some lines, keeping the most important and moving ones. Present your edited version and show how Ferdinand reacts when he sees his murdered niece and nephew. Does he react differently when he sees the body of his sister?

Pictures with captions: Draw pictures to illustrate three key moments: 1. 'Here begin your pity' (line 94); 2. 'The death of young wolves is never to be pitied' (lines 95–96); 3. 'Cover her face. Mine eyes dazzle. She died young' (line 101). Here is one example.

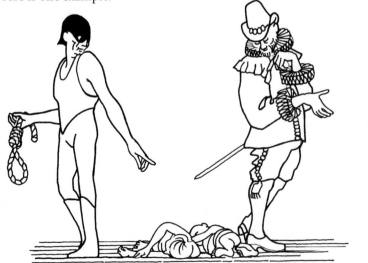

Caption: 'The death of young wolves is never to be pitied.'

Explanation: 'These children would kill me for revenge if I allowed them to live.'

CARIOLA   My turn is next,
            Is it not so ordered?
BOSOLA   Yes, and I am glad
            You are so well prepared for it.
CARIOLA   You are deceived sir,
            I am not prepared for it. I will not die,
            I will first come to my answer; and know   85
            How I have offended.
BOSOLA   Come, dispatch her.
            You kept her counsel. Now you shall keep ours.
CARIOLA   I will not die, I must not, I am contracted
            To a young gentleman.
BOSOLA   [showing the noose] Here's your wedding-ring.
CARIOLA   Let me but speak with the Duke. I'll discover   90
            Treason to his person.
BOSOLA   Delays: throttle her.
EXECUTIONER She bites: and scratches.
CARIOLA   I am quick with child.
BOSOLA   Why then,
            Your credit's saved: bear her into the next room.
            Let this lie still.

            Executioners strangle Cariola and leave carrying her body. Enter Ferdinand

FERDINAND   Is she dead?
BOSOLA   Here begin your pity,

            Bosola draws back a curtain to reveal the children strangled

            Alas, how have these offended?
FERDINAND   The death   95
            Of young wolves is never to be pitied.
BOSOLA   Fix your eye here.
FERDINAND   Constantly.
BOSOLA   Do you not weep?
            Other sins only speak. Murder shrieks out:
            The element of water moistens the earth,
            But blood flies upwards, and bedews the heavens.   100
FERDINAND   Cover her face. Mine eyes dazzle. She died young.
BOSOLA   I think not so. Her infelicity
            Seemed to have years too many.
FERDINAND   She and I were twins,
            And should I die this instant, I had lived
            Her time to a minute.   105

---

85 **come to my answer** be   88   **contracted** engaged to be   92 **quick with child** pregnant
answered   married   93 **credit** honour, reputation
86 **dispatch her** kill her   90–91 **discover treason to his**   102 **infelicity** unhappiness
87 **counsel** secrets, confidences   **person** reveal traitors
                                            against the Duke

The Murderer and his Wife

Macbeth and his wife plan to murder King Duncan and become rulers of Scotland in his place. When he visits their castle, they put their plan into action. After a night of drinking and celebration, everyone is sleeping. Lady Macbeth waits outside as Macbeth enters King Duncan's bedchamber intent on murder.

1 Is the deed done? (groups of four)

Lady Macbeth has been drinking, perhaps to give herself courage ('That which hath made them drunk, hath made me bold'). As she waits in the darkness, she hears someone call out (line 9) and fears the guards may have awakened and caught her husband in the act of murdering the King.

- Read lines 1–14 aloud, handing on to the next person at each punctuation mark. Try reading the lines in different ways: loudly and confidently, cruelly and aggressively, whispering fearfully.
- Decide on the best ways to speak different sections of these lines and then present a reading to the class showing Lady Macbeth's changing emotions.
- Study what Lady Macbeth says in these lines. What part did she play in ensuring (a) that the guards would be unconscious and (b) that they would be accused of the murder when King Duncan's body is discovered in the morning?

2 'My husband?' (in pairs)

It is dark. Macbeth has just stabbed the King to death. Memorise lines 13–24 (from 'Enter Macbeth with two bloody daggers' to 'A foolish thought to say a sorry sight'), then rehearse your version. Think about the following things:

ACTION 1: There is a question mark after 'My husband?' (line 13). What clue does that give you as to how Lady Macbeth behaves at that moment? Some editors print an exclamation mark ('My husband!') How should Lady Macbeth behave now?
ACTION 2: Decide why Macbeth says 'Hark!' (line 21) and how he should look at his hands (line 23).
HOW THEY SPEAK: Try different ways of speaking the lines: perhaps quickly and excitedly, with many fearful pauses, or whispering to each other for fear of being discovered.

When you show your version to the rest of the class, finish with a freeze/tableau to show the different states of mind of Macbeth and Lady Macbeth.

Macbeth by William Shakespeare (about 1606)

Act 2 scene 2 The Courtyard in Macbeth's castle

Enter Lady Macbeth

LADY MACBETH That which hath made them drunk, hath made me bold;
What hath quenched them, hath given me fire.

An owl shrieks

                       Hark, peace!
It was the owl that shrieked, the fatal bellman
Which gives the stern'st good-night. He is about it.
The doors are open, and the surfeited grooms   5
Do mock their charge with snores. I have drugged their possets,
That death and nature do contend about them,
Whether they live, or die.

MACBETH   [*Within*] Who's there? What, ho?

LADY MACBETH Alack, I am afraid they have awaked,
And 'tis not done. The attempt and not the deed   10
Confounds us. Hark! I laid their daggers ready,
He could not miss 'em. Had he not resembled
My father as he slept, I had done't.

Enter Macbeth with two bloody daggers

                     My husband?

MACBETH I have done the deed. Didst thou not hear a noise?

LADY MACBETH I heard the owl scream and the crickets cry.   15
Did not you speak?

MACBETH When?

LADY MACBETH Now.

MACBETH As I descended?

LADY MACBETH Ay.   20

MACBETH Hark! Who lies i' the second chamber?

LADY MACBETH Donalbain.

MACBETH This is a sorry sight. [*Looking on his hands*]

LADY MACBETH A foolish thought, to say a sorry sight.

---

2 **quenched** silenced
3 **fatal bellman** watchman who rings the bell before
  executions and burials
5 **surfeited grooms** drunken servants
6 **mock their charge** neglect their duties

6 **possets** hot drinks
7 **contend about them** fight it out between them
21 **chamber** bedroom
22 **Donalbain** King Duncan's son

3 The voice of Macbeth's conscience (in pairs)

From the moment that he murders the King, Macbeth realises what a terrible crime he has committed. In lines 25–32 he tells Lady Macbeth how he heard two sleepers (possibly the King's bodyguards) stir in their sleep and mutter a prayer to God. When they say 'God bless us', Macbeth, to his horror, finds he cannot pray with them. It is as if, in killing King Duncan, he has cut himself off from all goodness.

Read from line 25 to the end of the scene. Copy and continue this 'Conscience Chart' to explore Macbeth's fears and guilty feelings.

Macbeth's guilty conscience	
What he says	**What he feels**
'seen me with these hangman's hands'	He thinks he is like an executioner with his bloodstained hands
'I could not say "Amen" when they did say "God bless us"'	He thinks he can no longer look to God for help and comfort

When you have completed your chart, use it in one or both of the following ways.

- One of you speaks to the class in role as Macbeth. Tell them how the murder of King Duncan has affected you. The other speaks in role as Lady Macbeth. Tell them how the murder has affected you and your husband.
- Write Macbeth's secret diary in which he confesses his crime and expresses his guilty conscience.

4 'Methought I heard a voice cry, "Sleep no more!"' (small groups)

In lines 38–46, Macbeth imagines that he hears a voice crying loud enough to wake the whole castle, saying that he will never sleep again. Macbeth lists all the comforts that sleep can bring, comforts that he believes he will never enjoy again.

- Illustrate each comfort that sleep brings, with captions. Here is an example:

'Sleep that knits up the ravelled sleeve of care'

MACBETH   There's one did laugh in's sleep, and one cried 'Murder!'   25
           That they did wake each other; I stood and heard them,
           But they did say their prayers, and addressed them
           Again to sleep.
LADY MACBETH   There are two lodged together.
MACBETH   One cried 'God bless us!' and 'Amen' the other,
           As they had seen me with these hangman's hands.   30
           List'ning their fear, I could not say 'Amen'
           When they did say 'God bless us.'
LADY MACBETH   Consider it not so deeply.
MACBETH   But wherefore could not I pronounce 'Amen'?
           I had most need of blessing, and 'Amen'   35
           Stuck in my throat.
LADY MACBETH   These deeds must not be thought
           After these ways; so, it will make us mad.
MACBETH   Methought I heard a voice cry, 'Sleep no more:
           Macbeth does murder sleep', the innocent sleep,
           Sleep that knits up the ravelled sleeve of care,   40
           The death of each day's life, sore labour's bath,
           Balm of hurt minds, great nature's second course,
           Chief nourisher in life's feast.
LADY MACBETH   What do you mean?
MACBETH   Still it cried. 'Sleep no more' to all the house;
           'Glamis hath murdered sleep', and therefore Cawdor   45
           Shall sleep no more: Macbeth shall sleep no more.
LADY MACBETH   Who was it, that thus cried? Why, worthy thane,
           You do unbend your noble strength to think
           So brain-sickly of things. Go get some water
           And wash this filthy witness from your hand.   50
           Why did you bring these daggers from the place?
           They must lie there. Go carry them and smear
           The sleepy grooms with blood.
MACBETH   I'll go no more.
           I am afraid to think what I have done;
           Look on't again, I dare not.

25	in's in his	42	second course main course of a meal
27–8	addressed them again went back	45	Glamis, Cawdor (Macbeth was Lord of Glamis
30	hangman's hands blood-covered		and Cawdor)
40	ravelled sleeve frayed sleeve, or tangled silk	47	thane lord
41	sore labour's bath hard work's cure	48	unbend weaken
42	Balm healing medicine	53	grooms bodyguards, servants

5 Images of blood (individual or small groups)

Macbeth brings the guards' daggers with him when he leaves King Duncan's room (line 51). His wife tells him he should have left them there, but Macbeth seems frozen and can only look in horror at his blood-covered hands. There seems so much blood that not all the water in the ocean could wash his hands clean: more likely the blood on his hands would turn the green ocean blood-red.

Read the whole scene and (a) write down all the 'blood' words Macbeth and his wife use, or words where they refer to washing their hands clean (b) note the moments where the audience would be very aware of the blood.

6 'Whence is that knocking?' (groups of three or four)

The whole scene so far has been dark and quiet. Suddenly, at line 60, there is a tremendous hammering on the castle gates. Write your own shortened version of lines 55 to the end. Include key phrases from Shakespeare's script plus some of your own words. Two of you play the roles of Macbeth and Lady Macbeth. The others create the sound effects of the knocking at the gate.

7 Compare the murders of King Duncan and the Duchess of Malfi (small groups)

Shakespeare and Webster (see pages 34–41) create two very different murder scenes. Read through both scenes again and then record the differences on a chart like the one below.

	The Duchess of Malfi	Macbeth
Who is murdered? How?		
Where? On or off stage? What is the effect of this?		
How does the victim behave?		
How do the murderers behave?		
Where in the scene does the audience feel fear or horror?		
How do the murderers speak about the murders they commit?		
Do you feel sympathy for the victim? Give your reasons.		
Do you feel sympathy for the murderers? Give your reasons.		
Which murderer is the most evil and why? (Ferdinand, Bosola, Macbeth or Lady Macbeth?)		

Use the information your group has collected to write an essay comparing the murder scenes in *The Duchess of Malfi* and *Macbeth*.

LADY MACBETH   Infirm of purpose!   55
Give me the daggers. The sleeping and the dead
Are but as pictures; 'tis the eye of childhood
That fears a painted devil. If he do bleed,
I'll gild the faces of the grooms withal,
For it must seem their guilt.

Exit Lady Macbeth. Knocking within.

MACBETH   Whence is that knocking?   60
How is't with me, when every noise appals me?
What hands are here? Ha: they pluck out mine eyes.
Will all great Neptune's ocean wash this blood
Clean from my hand? No: this my hand will rather
The multitudinous seas incarnadine,   65
Making the green one red.

Re-enter Lady Macbeth

LADY MACBETH   My hands are of your colour, but I shame
To wear a heart so white.

Knocking within

                              I hear a knocking
At the south entry. Retire we to our chamber;
A little water clears us of this deed.   70
How easy is it then! Your constancy
Hath left you unattended.

Knocking within

                              Hark, more knocking.
Get on your night-gown, lest occasion call us
And show us to be watchers. Be not lost
So poorly in your thoughts.   75
MACBETH   To know my deed, 'twere best not know myself.

Knocking within

Wake Duncan with thy knocking: I would thou couldst.

Exeunt

55	**infirm of purpose** you weakling!	65	**multitudinous** vast
59	**gild … withal** paint the faces of the guards with King Duncan's blood	65	**incarnadine** make blood red
59	**withal** with it all (i.e. the blood)	71–72	**Your constancy … unattended** you have lost your nerve
63	**Neptune** god of the sea	73	**lest occasion call us** in case they look for us

LOVE AND MARRIAGE, ROGUES AND FOOLS
(late 17th- and 18th-century drama)

King Charles I is executed and all the public theatres are closed

In the middle of the 17th century, civil war broke out in England. The Roundheads and Puritans, who wanted England to be governed by Parliament rather than by the King, fought and defeated the forces of King Charles I. The Puritans hated the theatres, which they thought encouraged loose and immoral behaviour, so they closed down all the public theatres in England. King Charles I was executed.

Late 17th-century Restoration drama

The Puritans kept the public theatres closed for 18 years until they lost power and King Charles II was restored to the throne of England. The new king and his court loved the theatre, so new and entirely indoor theatres were built which were lit by artificial light (usually candles). The audiences were mainly the aristocracy and upper class who loved watching comedies with clever, elegant characters speaking sparkling, witty dialogue. Women could now act on stage and were very popular. Aphra Behn's play, *The Rover* (see pages 50–53), tells of the adventures of two very lively and independent young women. George Farquhar's *The Recruiting Officer* (see pages 54–61) also has a very determined young heroine.

Going to the theatre in the 18th century

When the wealthier middle classes became interested in going to see plays, more theatres were opened. These new theatres were generally oblong in shape with the audience at one end, as most theatres are today.

The acting area was in two parts: a stage for painted scenery at the back, and another much larger stage in front of it (called the proscenium) where the acting was done (see picture opposite). This helped the actors to get close to the audience if they wished to, rather like the actors on an Elizabethan stage (see pages 16–17).

The audience either sat on benches in a sloping 'pit' in front of the stage, in sloping tiers facing the stage, or in boxes in the side walls. Both the stage and the auditorium (audience area) were lit by candles.

It was very fashionable and quite respectable in the 18th century 'to be seen at a play', but going to the theatre was a rowdy and sometimes dangerous thing to do. Drunks were very common, and audiences often shouted out or talked during the performance. Many hooligans came to the theatre just to cause a disturbance. Riots sometimes broke out and men fought duels. Sir Andrew Stanning was killed as he came out of a theatre. In 1735, the actor Charles Macklin murdered his companion Hall by thrusting his stick into the other's eyes.

What 18th-century audiences loved to see

Comedy was still very popular in the 18th century. Plays often made fun of the way people behaved. Two favourite comic characters were the old woman trying to appear young and the jealous old man married to a young wife. Sir Peter Teazle in Sheridan's *The School for Scandal* (see pages 62–65) is one such old man.

However, there was also a new middle-class audience who wanted to see plays about real people like themselves. Merchants and other middle-class characters were now put into plays, not just to be laughed at, but as examples of people coping with everyday problems: family, marriage, personal behaviour.

This drawing shows a scene from Sheridan's play, *The School for Scandal*. Lady Teazle has been secretly seeing another man and has hidden behind a screen to avoid being discovered by her husband. The picture shows the moment when the screen falls down to reveal Lady Teazle's hiding place. You can see the scenery stage at the back with the very large acting stage in front. The audience would be in the pit at the front of the stage, on tiered seats , or in side boxes.

Feisty Young Women

There are very few female pre-20th-century dramatists and Aphra Behn is one of the best known of them. *The Rover* is her most popular play. It is set in Naples, Italy, and tells the story of Florinda, a Spanish lady who falls in love with a dashing English Colonel, Lord Belvile. Florinda's father, however, wants Florinda to marry the old but very rich Don Vincentio. Florinda's sister, Hellena, is training to be a nun but seems most unsuited to a religious life. When Hellena finds out that Florinda loves Belvile, she decides to find herself a lover too.

1 'How full of questions!' (in pairs)

The play opens with the two sisters, Hellena and Florinda, talking about men, love and marriage. Before you read this extract, study these pictures:

What do Florinda and Hellena say to each other?

'What an impertinent thing is a young Girl bred in a Nunnery! How full of Questions!'

'Now you have provided your self with a Man, you take no Care for poor me.'

Based only on what you learn from these pictures, write answers to the following:

- What does Hellena, the sister who is a novice nun, intend to do?
- Describe the characters of these two women. How like a nun is Hellena?
- What questions will Hellena ask her sister Florinda?

When you have written your notes, take a part each and read lines 1–37 to see if your predictions are correct.

The Rover or The Banished Cavaliers by Aphra Behn (1677)

Act 1 scene 1 Naples. Carnival time

A chamber. Enter Florinda and Hellena

FLORINDA	What an impertinent thing is a young Girl bred in a Nunnery! How full of Questions! Prithee no more, Hellena.
HELLENA	The more's my Grief; I would fain know as much as you, which makes me so inquisitive; nor is it enough to know you're a Lover, unless you tell me who 'tis you sigh for.

5

FLORINDA When you are a lover, I'll think you fit for a Secret of that nature.

HELLENA 'Tis true, I was never a Lover yet – but I fancy it very pretty to sigh, and sing, and blush and wish, and dream and wish, and long and wish to see the Man; and when I do, look pale and tremble; just as you did when my Brother brought home the fine English Colonel to see you – Don Belvile.

10

FLORINDA Fie, Hellena.

HELLENA That Blush betrays you – I am sure 'tis so. Or is it Don Antonio the Vice-Roy's Son? Or perhaps the rich old Don Vincentio, whom my father designs for your husband? Why do you blush again?

FLORINDA With Indignation; and how near soever my Father thinks I am to marrying that hated Object, I shall let him see I understand better what's due to my Beauty, Birth and Fortune, and more to my Soul, than to obey those unjust Commands.

15

HELLENA Now hang me, if I don't love thee for that dear Disobedience. I love Mischief strangely, as most of our Sex do. But tell me, dear Florinda, don't you love that fine Anglese? He is so handsome.

20

FLORINDA Hellena, a Maid designed for a Nun ought not to be so curious in a Discourse of Love.

HELLENA And dost thou think that ever I'll be a nun? Or at least till I'm so old, I'm fit for nothing else. Faith no, Sister; and that which makes me long to know whether you love Belvile, is because I hope he has some mad Companion. Nay I'm resolved to provide my self this Carnival, if there be a handsome Fellow of my Humour above Ground, though I ask first.

25

FLORINDA Prithee be not so wild.

HELLENA Now you have provided your self with a Man, you take no Care for poor me. Prithee tell me, what dost thou see about me that is unfit for Love – have not I a world of Youth? A Beauty passable? Well shaped? Clean limbed? Sweet breathed? And Sense enough to know how all these ought to be employed to the best advantage: yes, I do and will. Therefore lay aside your Hopes of my Fortune, by me being a Devotee, and tell me how you came acquainted with this Belvile; for I perceive you knew him before he came to Naples.

30

FLORINDA Yes, I knew him at the Siege of Pamplona. He was the Colonel who, when the Town was ransacked, nobly treated my Brother and my self. And I must own my Heart will suffer no other to enter – But see my Brother.

35

2	**Prithee** I beg you	20	**Anglese** Englishman	33	**Devotee** nun
3	**fain** gladly	21	**Discourse of** conversation about	35	**Pamplona** a town in Spain
11	**Fie** shame on you				
12	**Vice-Roy** Governor of country or province	26	**of my Humour** of a similar personality to me		

2 Hellena and Florinda challenge their brother and father (groups of three)

There are three men who admire Florinda. Here is an artist's impression of them:

1 *Colonel Belvile, the dashing English cavalier*

2 *Don Antonio, the Vice-Roy's self-important son*

3 *Rich, old Don Vincentio, who has the support of Florinda's father and brother*

Take a part each and read the whole extract. Write notes on the following.
- What the two sisters think of each man and of arranged marriages.
- What Don Pedro thinks are the advantages of marrying Don Vincentio.

3 How English has changed: a fashion for Capitals

The use of capital letters in this extract is different from what you are taught to do. Make a list of the words which would not have capitals today. Why do you think they used capitals like this in the late 17th century?

4 Roles on the wall (in pairs)

It is not surprising that a woman dramatist should present strong female characters. Show your opinions of Hellena and Florinda on a wall display.

Comment on their personality, the way they speak, their appearance, and how they should be played on stage. Include quotes from the play as evidence.

Enter Don Pedro, his servant Stephano, carrying carnival costume, and Callis, governess to the sisters

DON PEDRO Good morrow, Sister. Pray, when saw you your Lover Don Vincentio?

FLORINDA I know not, Sir – Callis, when was he here? For I consider it so little, I know not when it was.   40

DON PEDRO I have a Command from my Father here to tell you, you ought not to despise him, a Man of so vast a Fortune, and such a Passion for you – Stephano, my things.

Don Pedro puts on his Carnival Mask and Costume

FLORINDA A Passion for me! I hate Vincentio, and I would not have a man so dear to me as my Brother make a Slave of his sister – and Sir, my Father's Will, I'm sure you may divert.

DON PEDRO I know not how dear I am to you, but I wish only to be ranked in your Esteem,   45
equal with the English Colonel Belvile. Why do you frown and blush? Is there any Guilt belongs to the name of that Cavalier?

FLORINDA I'll not deny I value Belvile: when I was exposed to such Dangers as the licensed Lust of common Soldiers, when Rage and Conquest flew through the City – then Belvile threw himself into all Dangers to save my Honour, so will you not allow him   50
my Esteem?

DON PEDRO Yes, pay him what you will in Honour – but you must consider Don Vincentio's fortune, and the Jointure he'll make you.

FLORINDA Let him consider my Youth, Beauty and Fortune; which ought not to be thrown away on his Age and Jointure.   55

DON PEDRO 'Tis true, he's not so young and fine a Gentleman as that Belvile – but what Jewels will that Cavalier present you with? Those of his Eyes and Heart?

HELLENA And are not those better than any Don Vincentio has brought from the Indies?

DON PEDRO Why how now! Has your Nunnery-breeding taught you to understand the Value of Hearts and Eyes?   60

HELLENA Better than to believe Vincentio deserves Value from any woman. He may perhaps increase her Bags, but not her Family.

DON PEDRO Go up to your Devotion, you are not designed for the Conversation of Lovers.

HELLENA [*Aside*] Nor Saints yet a while I hope –
Is it not enough you make a Nun of me, but you must cast my Sister away too,   65
exposing her to a worse confinement than a religious Life?

DON PEDRO The Girl's mad! Is it a Confinement to be carried into the Country, to an ancient Villa belonging to the Family of the Vincentios these five hundred Years, and have no other Prospect than that pleasing one of seeing all her own that meets her Eyes – a fine Air, large Fields and Gardens, where she may walk and gather   70
Flowers?

HELLENA And this man you must kiss – and nuzzle thro his Beard to find his Lips – and this you must submit to for threescore Years, and all for a Jointure.

DON PEDRO For all your Character of Don Vincentio, she is as like to marry him as she was before.

---

44 **Father's Will** father's commands
48 **licensed Lust** authorised sexual assaults

53 **Jointure ... make you** money and property he'll leave you in his will

62 **increase her Bags ... Family** give her more wealth but no children

Silence in Court!

Dramatists have always liked making fun of people in authority and George Farquhar is no exception. In this courtroom scene, Captain Plume, the Recruiting Officer, and his assistant, Sergeant Kite, are in a small country town collecting recruits for the army by any means possible. Captain Plume flirts with the women so their broken-hearted boyfriends will enlist, while Kite pretends to be an astrologer to persuade men to sign up. In this scene, three Judges assess the recruits.

1   Knockabout comedy (groups of five)

The scene opens with the three judges, Balance, Scale and Scruple, taking their seats on the bench. Mr Constable, the court official, is explaining what is going on to Sergeant Kite. Rehearse and present your version of lines 1–18. Two take the parts of Sergeant Kite and Mr Constable, the others act as the three judges.

- The judges should enter solemnly, then Sergeant Kite and Mr Constable begin the comedy which ends with the constable being beaten over the head.
- Decide what kind of man Mr Constable is. Is he clever or stupid?

2 What's in a name? (in pairs)

Names are often important in comedy. They can provide clues to what a character will be like. Design a diagram like the one started below. Around each name draw or write the clues that a particular name gives about its owner. You may get helpful ideas from a large dictionary.

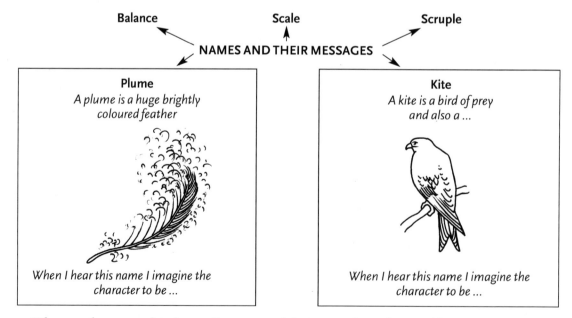

Balance   Scale   Scruple

NAMES AND THEIR MESSAGES

Plume
A plume is a huge brightly coloured feather

When I hear this name I imagine the character to be ...

Kite
A kite is a bird of prey and also a ...

When I hear this name I imagine the character to be ...

When you have completed your diagram, read the extract through to see if your first impressions were correct.

The Recruiting Officer by George Farquhar (1706)

Act 5 scene 5

*A Court of Law. **Justices Balance**, **Scale** and **Scruple** are the three judges on the bench; **Constable**, **Kite** and the Mob (members of the public) are in attendance; **Kite** and **Constable** move forward*

KITE   Pray, who are those honourable gentlemen upon the bench?

CONSTABLE   He in the middle is Justice Balance, he on the right is Justice Scale, and he on the left is Justice Scruple, and I am Mr Constable – four very honest gentlemen.

KITE   Sir, I am your most obedient servant [*Saluting the Constable*]. I fancy, sir, that your employment and mine are much the same; for my business is to keep   5 people in order, and if they disobey, to knock 'em down; and then we are both staff officers.

CONSTABLE   Nay, I'm a sergeant myself – of the militia. Come, brother, you shall see me exercise. Suppose this is a musket now. [*He puts his staff on his right shoulder*] Now I am shouldered.   10

KITE   Ay, you are shouldered pretty well for a constable's staff, but for a musket you must put it on the other shoulder, my dear.

CONSTABLE   Adso! That's true. Come, now give the word of command.

KITE   Silence!

CONSTABLE   Ay, ay, so we will. We will be silent.   15

KITE   Silence, you dog, silence! [*Strikes him over the head with his halberd*]

CONSTABLE   That's the way to silence a man with a witness! What d'ye mean, friend?

KITE   Only to exercise you, sir.

Enter Captain Plume

BALANCE   Captain, you're welcome.

PLUME   Gentlemen, I thank you.   20

SCRUPLE   Come, honest Captain, sit by me. [*Plume takes his seat upon the bench*] Now produce your prisoners. Here, that fellow there – set him up. [*The constable brings the prisoner into the dock*] Mr Constable, what have you to say against this man?

CONSTABLE   I have nothing to say against him, if it please you.

BALANCE   No! What made you bring him hither?   25

CONSTABLE   I don't know, if it please your worship.

SCRUPLE   Did not the contents of your warrant direct you what sort of men to take up?

CONSTABLE   I can't tell, if it please you, I can't read.

SCRUPLE   A very pretty constable truly! I find we have no business here.

KITE   May it please your worship, I desire to be heard in this case, as being   30 counsel for the Queen.

---

7 **staff officers** non-commissioned officers

9 **staff** stick or baton, symbol of authority

16 **halberd** a combination spear and battle-axe

17 **That's … with a witness** That really is a way to silence a man!

22 **set him up** put him in the dock

27 **warrant** official order to arrest someone

27 **take up** arrest

29 **I find … business here** this case does not concern us

31 **counsel** legal representative

3 How to get recruits for the army (groups of about four)

Recruiting officers like Plume used all sorts of devious plans to trick men into
enlisting: getting them drunk, bribery, exaggerating the glamour of military life,
and so on. Improvise your own scenes in which different men are
tricked/persuaded into joining the army (or perhaps just escape joining).

4 How fair is this Court of Law? (individual or small groups)

The Impressment Act was passed by Parliament to allow suitable men to be
'pressed' (forced or conscripted) into the armed forces. The most 'suitable' men
were usually either poor, unmarried, unemployed or criminal and they were
summoned to court (as they are in this scene) to see whether they were 'suitable
cases' for conscription. To ensure a fair trial, no military person was allowed to sit
in judgement on matters of conscription.

Read lines 19–54 where the judges deal with the first prisoner. What examples of
unjust or biased behaviour by the judges, Plume and Kite can you find?

5 Show how the first prisoner loses his case (large groups or whole class)

The first candidate for conscription is brought into court but never gets the
chance to defend himself – in fact he never says a word! Rehearse and
present your version of lines 19–54.

- Set up your courtroom with the three judges and Plume
  presiding. You will need the Constable and the silent
  first prisoner as well as Sergeant Kite.
- Remember to create the Public Gallery. The
  prisoner's wife is there, probably with
  friends and relatives who make their
  feelings felt during the course of the
  trial (the stage directions call
  them a 'mob').
- The one playing the part
  of the silent prisoner
  could speak his
  thoughts at the end,
  just before he is taken
  away.

BALANCE   Come, Sergeant, you shall be heard. We won't come here for nothing.

KITE   This man is but one man; the country may spare him, and the army wants him; besides, he's cut out by nature for a grenadier; he's five foot ten inches high; he gets drunk every sabbath day, and he beats his wife.   35

WIFE   You lie, sirrah, you lie! if it please your worship, he's the best-natur'dst, pains-taking'st man in the parish, witness my five poor children.

SCRUPLE   A wife and five children! You, Constable, you rogue, how durst you impress a man that has a wife and five children?

SCALE   Discharge him! Discharge him!   40

BALANCE   Hold, gentlemen! Hark'ee friend, how do you maintain your wife and five children?

KITE   The husband keeps a gun, and kills all the hares and partridges within five miles round.

BALANCE   A gun! Nay, if he be so good at gunning, he may be of use against the French.   45

SCRUPLE   But his wife and children, Mr Balance!

WIFE   Ay, ay, that's the reason you would send him away; you know I have a child every year, and you are afraid I should come upon the parish at last.

PLUME   Look'ee there, gentlemen, the honest woman has spoke it at once; the parish had better maintain five children this year, than six or seven the next.   50

WIFE   Look'ee, Mr Captain, the parish shall get nothing by sending him away, for I won't lose my teeming-time if there be a man left in the parish.

BALANCE   Send that woman to the house of correction – and the man –

KITE   I'll take care of him, if you please.   [*Kite takes the prisoner down*]

SCALE   Here, you Constable, the next: set up that black-faced fellow, he has a gunpowder look. [*The Constable brings the Second Prisoner to the dock*] What can you say against this man, Constable?   55

CONSTABLE   Nothing, but that he is a very honest man.

PLUME   Pray, gentlemen, let me have one honest man in my company for the novelty's sake.   60

BALANCE   What are you, friend?

2ND PRISONER   A collier, I work in the coal-pits.

SCRUPLE   Look'ee, gentlemen, this fellow has a trade, and the Act of Parliament expresses, that we are to impress no man that has any visible means of a livelihood.

KITE   May it please your worships, this man has no visible means of livelihood, for he works underground.   65

PLUME   Well said, Kite! Besides, the army wants miners.

BALANCE   Right, and had we an order of government for it, we could raise you five hundred colliers, that would run you underground like moles, and do more service in a siege than all the miners in the army.   70

---

35 **sabbath-day** Sunday

36 **sirrah** a rude way to address a man

37 **pains-taking** careful and conscientious

38, 64 **impress** force to enlist in the army

48 **I should ... parish** the parish would have to support me

52 **my teeming-time** time when I can get pregnant

53 **house of correction** place of punishment

56 **gunpowder look** looks as if he knows about guns

6 Fast talk (groups of seven)

The trial of the second prisoner, a coal-miner ('that black-faced fellow'), proceeds quickly with many short, sharp exchanges of words. The judges and Captain Plume have wasted enough time and want to get on with conscripting.

Take a part each and read lines 55–84 aloud. Speak your lines with pace and energy. Concentrate on Sergeant Kite's quick-witted replies to the second prisoner and his wife's pleas for mercy and consideration. You might record your performance on tape as a radio play.

7 Sergeant Kite, the sharp thinker (large groups or whole class)

Sergeant Kite is largely responsible for the second prisoner being conscripted. He has an answer to every argument the second prisoner and his wife put forward.

Rehearse your version of the second prisoner's trial (lines 55–84). Emphasise Kite's wit and the amused reactions of Plume and the judges to what he says. Some of you play the spectators in the public gallery. Do you laugh at Kite too? In the stage directions at the start of this scene, the spectators are described as a 'mob'. What part will the constable play in dealing with this mob?

8 Dramatic irony: we know something you don't know!

Dramatists often like to let their audience into secrets. A character will sometimes say something without realising its full meaning. This is called *dramatic irony*.

In this scene, Silvia, the daughter of Justice Balance, has disguised herself as Mr Pinch. Silvia is so madly in love with Captain Plume that she wants to be conscripted into the army to be with him. None of the characters on stage know this.

- Collect examples from lines 85–122 of dramatic irony (where a character says or does something which has a different meaning when you know all the facts).
- Divide your examples into (a) serious or moving (b) amusing moments of dramatic irony. Give reasons for your choices.

SCRUPLE   Well, friend, what have you to say for yourself?

2ND PRISONER   I'm married.

KITE   Lack-a-day, so am I!

2ND PRISONER   Here's my wife, poor woman.

BALANCE   Are you married, good woman?   75

WOMAN   I'm married in conscience.

KITE   May it please your worship, she's with child in conscience.

SCALE   Who married you, mistress?

WOMAN   My husband – we agreed that I should call him husband to avoid passing for a whore, and that he should call me wife, to shun going for a soldier.   80

SCRUPLE   A very pretty couple! Pray, Captain, will you take 'em both?

PLUME   What say you, Mr Kite? Will you take care of the woman?

KITE   Yes, sir; she shall go with us to the seaside, and there, if she has a mind to drown herself, we'll take care that nobody shall hinder her.

Kite takes down second Prisoner

BALANCE   Here, Constable, bring in my man. [*Exit Constable*] Now, Captain, I'll fit you   85
with a man, such as you never listed in your life. [*Enter Constable with Silvia*]

SCALE   Where is your respect to the bench?

SILVIA   Sir, I don't care a farthing for you nor your bench neither.

SCRUPLE   Look'ee, gentlemen, he's a very impudent fellow, and fit for a soldier.

SCALE   A notorious rogue, I say, and very fit for a soldier.   90

CONSTABLE   A whoremaster, I say, and therefore fit to go.

BALANCE   What think you, Captain?

PLUME   I think he's a very pretty fellow, and therefore fit to serve.

SILVIA   Send your own lazy, lubberly sons at home, fellows that hazard their necks every day in pursuit of a fox, yet dare not look an enemy in the face.   95

CONSTABLE   May it please your worships, I have a woman at the door to swear a rape against this rogue.

SILVIA   Is it your wife or daughter, booby? I ravished 'em both yesterday.

BALANCE   Pray, Captain, read the Articles of War, we'll see him listed immediately.

PLUME   [*Reads*] 'Articles of War against mutiny and desertion ...'   100

SILVIA   Hold, sir! Once more, gentlemen, have a care what you do, for you shall severely smart for any violence you offer to me; and you, Mr Balance, I speak to you particularly, you shall heartily repent it.

PLUME   Look'ee, young spark, say but one word more and I'll build a horse for you as high as the ceiling, and make you ride the most tiresome journey that   105
you ever made in your life.

SILVIA   You have made a fine speech, good Captain Huffcap, but you had better be quiet; I shall find a way to cool your courage.

---

76 **in conscience**   in spirit (not in fact)

80 **whore**   prostitute, loose woman

80 **shun ... soldier**   avoid being called up

86, 99 **listed**   enlisted

91 **whoremaster**   manager of a brothel

94 **lubberly**   clumsy, lazy, stupid

98 **booby**   fool

98 **ravished**   raped

99 **Articles of War**   the rules soldiers must obey

104–5 **horse ... as the ceiling**   a punishment device that soldiers had to sit astride

107 **Huffcap**   a flashy fighter

9 Act like a man! (groups of about ten)

Much of the comedy of Silvia's trial is seeing a young woman pretending to be a rude young man. Rehearse and present your version of lines 85–122. Consider:

- The different ways Silvia could imitate a rude young man – the way she speaks, sits or responds to questions. How does she behave towards Captain Plume, the man she loves?
- How the Justices, Plume and the spectators in the public gallery react to the sight of a young man behaving so rebelliously.

10 The twist in the tail (groups of about ten)

In comedies, justice usually triumphs. In this scene, the corrupt Constable, who has been taking bribes from men hoping to avoid being drafted into the army, finds himself caught out.

Rehearse lines 123–144. Concentrate on showing the Constable's horror as his crimes are revealed and he finds himself in the hands of Sergeant Kite, who hit him round the head at the start of this scene. The spectators express approval/disapproval as the Constable is taken away.

11 How does Farquhar make us laugh? (individual or groups)

Comedy works in many ways. The spider diagram below shows some of the ways Farquhar sets out to amuse us. Complete the diagram, adding other sections of your own if you wish. Use your diagram and notes to write an essay on the different kinds of comedy in *The Recruiting Officer*.

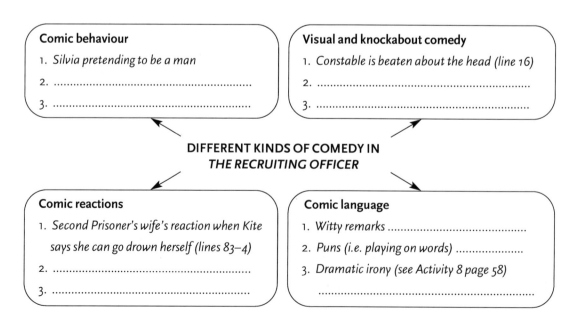

Comic behaviour

1. *Silvia pretending to be a man*
2. ....
3. ....

Visual and knockabout comedy

1. *Constable is beaten about the head (line 16)*
2. ....
3. ....

DIFFERENT KINDS OF COMEDY IN
THE RECRUITING OFFICER

Comic reactions

1. *Second Prisoner's wife's reaction when Kite says she can go drown herself (lines 83–4)*
2. ....
3. ....

Comic language

1. *Witty remarks* ....
2. *Puns (i.e. playing on words)* ....
3. *Dramatic irony (see Activity 8 page 58)*

....

PLUME	Pray, gentlemen, don't mind him, he's distracted.
SILVIA	'Tis false! I am descended of as good a family as any in your county; 110 my father is as good a man as any upon your bench.
BALANCE	He's certainly mad! Pray, Captain, read the Articles of War.
SILVIA	Hold, once more! Pray, Mr Balance, to you I speak; suppose I were your child, would you use me at this rate?
BALANCE	No, faith, were you mine, I would send you to Bedlam first, and into the 115 army afterwards.
SILVIA	But consider my father, sir, he's as good, as generous, as brave, as just a man as ever served his country; I'm his only child. The loss of me may break his heart.
BALANCE	He's a very great fool if it does. Captain, if you don't list him this minute I'll leave the court. 120
PLUME	Kite, do you distribute the levy-money to the men while I read.
KITE	Ay, sir. Silence, gentlemen!

Plume reads the Articles of War to swear them in as soldiers

BALANCE	Very well; now, Captain, let me beg the favour of you, not to discharge this fellow upon any account whatsoever. Bring in the rest.
CONSTABLE	There are no more, if it please your worship. 125
BALANCE	No more! There were five two hours ago.
SILVIA	'Tis true, sir, but this rogue of a constable let the rest escape for a bribe of eleven shillings a man.
ALL JUSTICES	How!
SILVIA	Gentlemen, he offered to let me get away for two guineas, but I had not 130 so much about me, this is truth, and I'm ready to swear it.
2ND PRISONER	May it please your worship, I gave him half-a-crown to say that I was an honest man; but now since that your worships have made me a rogue, I hope I shall have my money again.
BALANCE	'Tis my opinion that this constable be put into the captain's hands, and 135 if his friends don't bring four good men for his ransom by tomorrow night – Captain, you shall carry him to Flanders.
SCALE/SCRUPLE	Agreed, agreed!
PLUME	Mr Kite, take the constable into custody.
KITE	Ay, ay, sir. [*To Constable*] Will you please to have your office taken from you? 140 Or will you handsomely lay down your staff, as your betters have done before you?

The Constable drops his staff

BALANCE	Come, gentlemen, there needs no great ceremony in adjourning this court – Captain, you shall dine with me.
KITE	Come Mr Militia Serjeant, I shall silence you now, I believe.

Kite marches the Constable from the court

---

109 distracted mad
114 use me at this rate treat me in this way
115 Bedlam a lunatic asylum in London

121 levy-money money paid to men on joining the army
128 shillings, 130 guineas, 132 half-a-crown coins, money

137 Flanders Belgium
141 lay down your staff resign your position

Wedded Bliss

Dramatists have always enjoyed showing husbands and wives quarrelling. You may have already studied the extract from the 14th-century mystery play about Noah and the trouble he had with his wife (pages 8–11). In *The School for Scandal* by Sheridan there is another famous bickering couple. Sir Peter Teazle, an old man, has recently married. His young country-bred wife, Lady Teazle, is dazzled by fashionable London society, especially Lady Sneerwell and her friends (the 'School for Scandal') who spend their time spreading malicious gossip and rumours.

1 Is fashion important? (groups of four)

Lady Teazle certainly thinks fashion is important. Her husband is more concerned that she does not spend so much money! Is keeping in fashion as important as Lady Teazle thinks? Choose one of the following activities.

- Create an improvisation in which two teenagers ask their parents for the latest fashion accessory. The parents are not so sure that this item is either needed or affordable! The teenagers can make notes on the kinds of arguments and methods of persuasion they might use, while the parents make notes on the counter-arguments they could employ.
- Debate the importance of fashion. Two of you make notes giving reasons why keeping up with fashion is important. The other two make notes arguing against the importance of fashion (for example, 'what you are is more important than what you wear', 'comfort is better than fashion'). Use your notes to prepare speeches arguing your different points of view.

2 Lady Teazle gives her views on fashion (in pairs)

Why is Lady Teazle so concerned about being fashionable? Read through the whole extract, taking a part each. Make a note of the reasons she gives for being fashionable. Think about the following points:
- the life she led before she married Sir Peter
- her life now and the sort of friends she has (especially Lady Sneerwell).

Use your notes to prepare a presentation in role as Lady Teazle explaining why you behave as you do.

3 Be a bickering married couple (groups of eight)

Perform lines 1–42. As a group, divide into pairs. Each pair takes one of the following blocks of lines each: (a) lines 1–10 (b) lines 11–21 (c) lines 22–32 (d) lines 33–43. Learn your lines and rehearse them. Behave as if you are a very irritable married couple. Finish your section by creating a *tableau* (a frozen moment). When all four pairs are ready, show the whole section.

The School for Scandal by Richard Brinsley Sheridan (1777)

Act 2 scene 1   Sir Peter Teazle's house

Enter Sir Peter and Lady Teazle

SIR PETER Lady Teazle – Lady Teazle, I'll not bear it.

LADY TEAZLE Sir Peter – Sir Peter, you may bear it or not as you please, but I ought to have my own way in every thing, and what's more I will too – what! Though I was educated in the country, I know very well that women of Fashion in London are accountable to nobody after they are married. **5**

SIR PETER Very well! Ma'am very well! So a husband is to have no influence, no authority?

LADY TEAZLE Authority! No to be sure – if you wanted authority over me you should have adopted me and not married me. I am sure you were Old enough.

SIR PETER Old enough! Ay there it is – well – well, Lady Teazle, though my Life may be made unhappy by your Temper, I'll not be ruined by your extravagance. **10**

LADY TEAZLE My extravagance! I'm sure I'm not more extravagant than a woman of Fashion ought to be.

SIR PETER No no, Madam, you shall throw away no more sums on such unmeaning Luxury. 'Slife! To spend as much to furnish your Dressing Room with Flowers in winter, as would suffice to turn the Pantheon into a Green-house! **15**

LADY TEAZLE Lord! Sir Peter, am I to blame because Flowers are dear in cold weather? You should find fault with the Climate and not with me.

SIR PETER Oons! Madam – if you had been born to this I shouldn't Wonder at your talking thus – but you forget what your situation was when I married you.

LADY TEAZLE No – no – I don't, 'twas a very disagreeable one or I should never have married you. **20**

SIR PETER Yes – yes madam, you were then in somewhat an humbler Style – the Daughter of a plain country Squire. Recollect Lady Teazle when I saw you first – sitting at your tambour in a pretty figured Linnen gown – with a Bunch of Keys by your side, your hair combed smooth over a Roll, and your apartment hung around **25** with Fruits in worsted of your own working.

LADY TEAZLE O yes, I remember it very well, and a Curious life I led! My daily occupation to inspect the Dairy, superintend the Poultry, and Comb my aunt Deborah's Lap-Dog.

SIR PETER Yes, yes, Ma'am, 'twas so indeed.

LADY TEAZLE And then you know my evening amusements – to play Pope Joan with the **30** Curate – to read a Novel to my Aunt – or to be stuck down to an old Spinnet, to strum my Father to sleep after a Fox chase.

SIR PETER I am glad you have so good a Memory. Yes. Madam, these were the Recreations I took you from. But now you must have your Coach, and three powdered Footmen before your Chair – no Recollection I suppose when you were **35** content to ride double behind the Butler on a docked Coach Horse?

13	**unmeaning** pointless	24	**tambour** embroidery frame	30	**Pope Joan** a card game
15	**suffice** be enough	24	**figured** embroidered,	31	**Spinnet** musical instrument
13, 18	**'Slife! / Oons!** My God!		decorated		like a piano
15	**Pantheon** large concert	25	**Roll** padding put under the hair	35	**Chair** sedan chair
	hall in London	26	**worsted ... own working** cloth	36	**docked** with clipped tail
			you had woven yourself		

4 The put-down (groups of three)

People have differing ideas as to how Sir Peter and Lady Teazle should speak lines 38–46. Is Sir Peter sad, serious or joking when he says that Lady Teazle hopes he will die soon (line 42)? Is the noise Lady Teazle makes in reply ('Hem! Hem!') meant to sound hard-hearted, embarrassed, scornful – or what?

Two of you take the parts of Sir Peter and Lady Teazle and rehearse lines 38–46 in different ways. The third person acts as director, advising on how Sir Peter and his wife should speak and behave towards the other.

5 Sneerwell, Surface, Snake, Crabtree, Backbite and Candour (small groups)

The names in this play are often meant to suggest something of their owner's character. Sir Peter and Lady Teazle are two such names. Both seem to get pleasure from teasing or provoking each other (a teazle is a plant rather like a giant prickly thistle). Here is one artist's illustration of Sir Peter and Lady Teazle's name:

At the end of this scene, Lady Teazle leaves to take tea with Lady Sneerwell and her malicious friends. Here are the names of some of this group:

Lady Sneerwell   Joseph Surface
Mr Snake   Mr Crabtree
Mrs Candour   Sir Benjamin
                  Backbite

Write descriptions and draw pictures of how you imagine each of the above characters to be. Add speech bubbles showing the sorts of things you think each would say. If you want to know what these people are like in *The School for Scandal*, read the next scene of the play (Act 2 scene 2).

LADY TEAZLE	No – I swear I never did that. I deny the Butler, and the Coach Horse.
SIR PETER	This madam was your Situation – and what have I not done for you? I have made you a woman of Fashion, of Fortune, of Rank. In short I have made you my Wife.
LADY TEAZLE	Well then and there is but one thing more you can make me to add to the obligation – and that is –
SIR PETER	My widow I suppose?
LADY TEAZLE	Hem! Hem!
SIR PETER	Thank-you Madam, but don't flatter yourself. For though your ill conduct may disturb my Peace it shall never break my Heart. I promise you. However, I am equally obliged to you for the Hint.
LADY TEAZLE	Then why will you endeavour to make yourself so disagreeable to me, and thwart me in every little elegant expense?
SIR PETER	'Slife – Madam I say, had you any of these Elegant expenses when you married me?
LADY TEAZLE	Lud, Sir Peter, would you have me be out of the Fashion?
SIR PETER	The Fashion indeed! What had you to do with the Fashion before you married me?
LADY TEAZLE	I should think you would like to have your Wife thought a Woman of Taste.
SIR PETER	Aye, there again – Taste! Zounds Madam you had no Taste when you married me.
LADY TEAZLE	That's very true indeed Sir Peter and after having married you I am sure I should never pretend to Taste again! But now Sir Peter if we have finished our daily Jangle I presume I may go to my Engagement at Lady Sneerwell's.
SIR PETER	Aye – a charming set of acquaintance you have made there.
LADY TEAZLE	Nay, Sir Peter, they are People of Rank and Fortune – and remarkably tenacious of Reputation.
SIR PETER	Yes, 'egad, they are tenacious of Reputation with a vengeance, for they don't choose anybody should have a Character – but themselves. Such a crew! Ah! Many a wretch has rid on a hurdle who has done less mischief than those utterers of forged Tales, coiners of Scandal, and clippers of Reputation.
LADY TEAZLE	What would you restrain the freedom of speech?
SIR PETER	Oh! They have made you just as bad as any one of the Society.
LADY TEAZLE	Why – I vow I have no malice against the People I abuse, but Sir Peter you know you promised to come to Lady Sneerwell's too.
SIR PETER	Well well I'll call in just to look after my own character.
LADY TEAZLE	Then indeed you must make Haste after me or you'll be too late – so good bye to ye.

Exit Lady Teazle

SIR PETER	So - I have gained much by my intended expostulations - yet with what a charming air she contradicts every thing I say. Well, though I can't make her love me, there is a great Satisfaction in quarrelling with her and I think she never appears to such advantage as when she's doing every thing in her Power to plague me.

Exit Sir Peter Teazle

---

39 Rank high position in society
49, 50, 53, 60 'Slife! Lud! Zounds! 'egad swear words
56 Jangle row, argument

62 rid on a hurdle been sent to his execution
63 coiners and clippers forgers and cheaters

65 the Society i.e. 'The School for Scandal'
70 expostulations expressions of my disapproval

MELODRAMA AND WIT
(19th-century drama)

Victorian theatres and the working class

During the 18th century, usually only wealthy people could afford to go to the theatre. Besides, performances were in the afternoon or very early evening, when ordinary working people were still at work in the factories or shops.

In the 19th century, many more theatres were built. When the cheaper seats began to be bought by working-class people, the times of performances were changed to suit the new audience. Theatres now opened at about 6.30 p.m. and several different shows were put on throughout the evening. Workers who finished late could watch the second or third performance of the evening. As more and more working people went to the theatre, so the rich upper classes turned instead to the opera or ballet.

Victorian melodrama

After a hard day's work, a Victorian working-class audience enjoyed watching plenty of exciting action and lively songs. They wanted plays full of emotion and with happy endings. They particularly enjoyed the new melodramas: plays with a simple plot, a young handsome hero, a maiden in distress and a wicked villain. The acting was often exaggerated and the audience hissed at the villain, felt sorry for the heroine, laughed at the comic scenes and smiled when everything ended happily.

Melodramas were at first set in exotic foreign places with ghosts and bandits. Later, they were often set in the country in present-day times, with an evil squire and a rustic country boy as the hero. Some plays were based on stories by Charles Dickens, like *Oliver Twist*. Others were based on real-life sensational crime stories like the murder of Maria Marten in the Red Barn (see pages 68–75).

The rise of the Victorian music hall

In the second half of the 19th century, the music hall took over from the theatre as the place where most working people went to relax after a hard day's work. They came to listen to songs like 'A Bicycle Made for Two' and 'Two Lovely Black Eyes' and to join in with the choruses. Besides singers, there were a variety of acts to watch: acrobats, jugglers, dancers, ventriloquists and comedians.

Late 19th-century theatres

As working people began to go to the music hall for their entertainment, so theatres tried to tempt back the richer and more educated classes. Smaller theatres were built and just one high-quality production was put on each evening.

Gilbert and Sullivan's comic operas, like *The Mikado* and *The Pirates of Penzance*, were very popular, as were the witty plays of Oscar Wilde, like *The Importance of Being Earnest* (see pages 100–111).

Watching a play in Victorian times

During the 18th century, the large apron stage in front of the scenery stage had been gradually pushed further and further back, so more seats could be fitted in. By the 19th century, the stage and its scenery looked rather like a three-dimensional picture in a frame (see picture below). Many theatres today still have this design.

Productions went to great lengths to create a sense of realism on these 'picture frame' stages. There were huge painted backcloths and skilfully constructed scenery. Boats moved about on stage, actors would ride real horses. In a forest scene the audience would sometimes notice real rabbits hopping about.

Gas lights replaced candles in the early 19th century. If you burnt a stick of lime in a gas flame you could direct a single beam of light onto an actor or one part of the stage. This was the beginning of modern stage lighting and is the origin of the phrase 'in the limelight'. Gas lights were much brighter and could be better controlled, but were extremely dangerous and smelt terrible. Theatres quite often burnt down!

Villains and Victims

Maria Marten is one of the best-known Victorian melodramas. The villainous William Corder, son of the local squire, first makes Maria Marten pregnant, then secretly poisons the new-born child and persuades Maria to help him bury it in the wood. This extract begins at the point where Corder and Maria meet at the Red Barn ready to run away to London to be married. But Corder has other plans for Maria!

The play is based on a true story. William Corder murdered Maria Marten in 1827 and fled to London after hiding her body in the Red Barn. He was arrested after Maria appeared to her mother several times in a vision. The Red Barn was searched and Maria's body found. Ten thousand people turned out to watch Corder hang and his skeleton is still preserved in the courthouse of Bury St Edmunds along with an account of the trial bound in Corder's own skin.

1 What is melodrama? (groups of about six)

Perhaps the most famous image of melodrama is from the early cinema films where the evil villain in black cloak, hat and moustache ties the helpless heroine to the railway lines in the path of an approaching train. The hero defeats the villain's plans and rescues the heroine just in time. Here are some of the things that make up a typical Victorian melodrama:

- stock characters: villain, heroine/hero, and comedian
- exciting or spectacular scenes: murders, fights, ghosts, visions, punishments
- high emotions: fear, sadness, anger, outrage, happiness
- exaggerated drama: plenty of chances for actors to show their acting 'skills'
- music for a character or mood: villain's music, heroine's music, sad music
- a moral: the audience can go away feeling they have learned a lesson about life.

Take parts each and read the four scenes in this extract (pages 69–75). Then collect examples from these scenes of the elements of Victorian melodrama listed above. Put them onto a spider diagram like the one below.

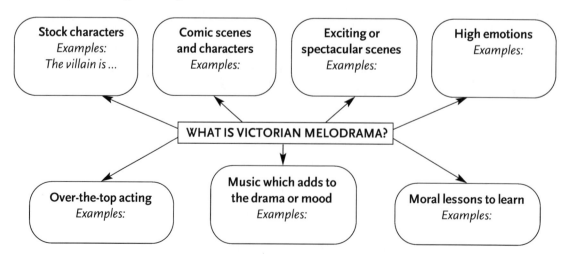

Maria Marten or The Murder in the Red Barn (1840)

Act 3 scene 3   Inside the Red Barn

William Corder is digging a grave. Villain's music

CORDER   All is complete, I await now my victim. Will she come? Oh yes, a woman is fool enough to do anything for the man she loves. Hark, 'tis her footstep bounding across the fields! She comes, with hope in her heart, a song on her lips, little does she think that death is so near.

He steps into a dark corner. Enter Maria Marten. The music turns soft and gentle

MARIA   William is not here. Where can he be? What ails me? A weight is in my heart   5
as if it told some evil, and this old barn how like a vault it looks. Fear steals upon me, I tremble in every limb. I will return to my home at once.

CORDER   [*moving towards Maria*] Stay, Maria!

MARIA   I'm glad you are here! You don't know how frightened I've been.

CORDER   Did any one see you cross the fields?   10

MARIA   Not a soul. I remembered your instructions.

CORDER   That's good. Now Maria do you remember a few days ago threatening to betray me about the child to Constable Ayers? [*Tremolo fiddles*]

MARIA   A girlish threat made in the heat of temper, because you refused to do justice to one you had wronged so greatly. Do not speak of that now, let   15
us leave this place.

CORDER   Not yet Maria, you don't think my life is to be held at the bidding of a silly girl. No! Look what I have made here!

He drags her to the grave. Slow music

MARIA   A grave! Oh, William, what do you mean?

CORDER   To kill you, bury your body here [*Corder points to the open grave*]. You are a   20
clog upon my actions, a chain that keeps me from reaching ambitious height. You are to die.

MARIA   [*kneels*] But not by your hand, the hand that I have clasped in love and confidence. Oh! Think William, how much I have sacrificed for you, think of our little child above, now in heaven pleads for its mother's life. Oh spare, oh spare me!   25

CORDER   'Tis useless, my mind's resolved, you die tonight.

Thunder crashes and lightning flashes

MARIA   Wretch!
Since neither prayers nor tears will touch your stony heart,
Heaven will surely nerve my arm to battle for my life.

Maria seizes Corder and fights for her life

CORDER   Foolish girl, desist!   30

MARIA   Never with life!

They struggle, he shoots her, she collapses in his arms

---

13   **Tremolo fiddles**   violin played with a quavering sound   21   **clog**   heavy weight

2 Behave like a character in Victorian melodrama (in pairs)

Actors in Victorian melodramas often used particular gestures and poses to express different emotions. Here are examples of some of them.

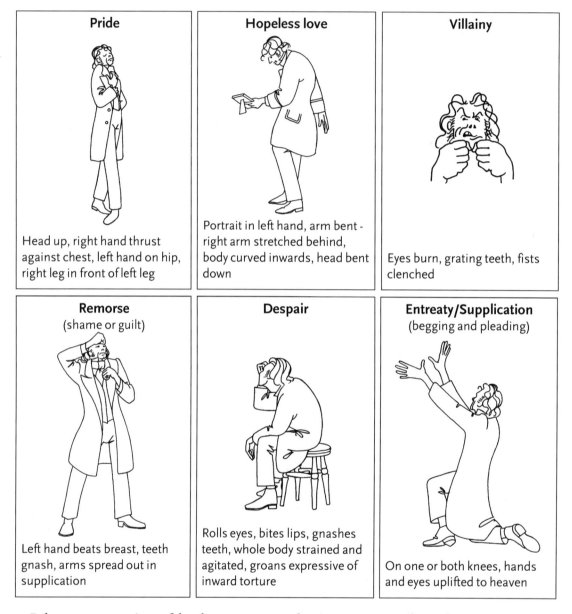

Pride

Head up, right hand thrust against chest, left hand on hip, right leg in front of left leg

Hopeless love

Portrait in left hand, arm bent - right arm stretched behind, body curved inwards, head bent down

Villainy

Eyes burn, grating teeth, fists clenched

Remorse
(shame or guilt)

Left hand beats breast, teeth gnash, arms spread out in supplication

Despair

Rolls eyes, bites lips, gnashes teeth, whole body strained and agitated, groans expressive of inward torture

Entreaty/Supplication
(begging and pleading)

On one or both knees, hands and eyes uplifted to heaven

Rehearse your versions of the above gestures and actions. Join up with another pair and see if they can guess the emotions you are showing. Then present a silent version of the murder scene from *Maria Marten* (Act 3 scene 3 pages 69–71) using melodramatic gestures and actions.

MARIA [*soft music*]
    William I am dying, your cruel hand has stilled
    The heart that beat in love alone for thee.
    Think not to escape the hand of justice, for
    When least expected it will mark you down,   **35**
    At that moment think of Maria's wrongs.
Death claims me, and with my final breath I die blessing and forgiving thee.

She dies

CORDER Blessing and forgiveness for me, her [*loud music*] murderer! What have I done! Oh, Maria, awake, awake! Let indignation lighten from your eyes and blast me!

    Oh may this crime for ever stand accurst,   **40**
    The last of murders, and it is the worst.

The story continues: *The spirit of the murdered Maria appears to her mother to tell her of the murder. The Red Barn is searched and Maria's grave discovered along with Corder's pistol. Pharos Lee hunts down Corder in London. He is arrested, tried and condemned to death.*

Act 5 scene 3:   A prison cell

CORDER So ends my dream of wealth. Tried, condemned today to be executed. Hundreds are flocking now to see me suspended between heaven and earth, the murderer's doom. Since my trial, night after night have I tried to sleep, but 'twas denied me. But now, when sleep eternal rapidly approaches in the form of death, my eyes grow weary, my eyelids close on this world of misery and thought.   **5**

Corder's head drops. He falls asleep. Maria appears

MARIA William, look on the murdered form of the girl who loved you. The last dread act of justice is about to be dealt upon thee. You thought to escape its power but the all-seeing eye was on your every action. Farewell, I shall be near thee on the scaffold.

Maria exits. Corder wakes up with a start

CORDER Away, away! I dare not gaze upon that ghastly form. 'Tis gone, a dream! How terrible!

    Such undistinguished horrors make my brain   **10**
    Like Hell the seat of darkness and of pain.

Enter Pharos Lee, the policeman

LEE Prisoner, the hour of execution is at hand but an old man wishes to speak with you.

5.3:2 suspended hanging on a rope   **5.3:8 scaffold** raised wooden platform used for hanging criminals

3 A melodramatic performance of Maria Marten (pairs and small groups)

Divide the extracts from *Maria Marten* into sections and rehearse and perform all four scenes in the style of a Victorian melodrama. Memorise your lines and find suitable music/sound effects. Make your finished presentation really heart-wrenching!

Act 3 scene 3 – The Murder (three pairs)

Divide into three sections of about 15–20 lines. Each pair freezes at the end of their section to allow the next pair to take over the performance.

Act 5 scene 3 – In the Prison Cell (three groups of three)

Divide into three sections (lines 1–8, 9–17, 18–49). Each group takes a section. Two of the group play the named parts and the other acts as director, advising them how to speak and move. In the second section (lines 9–17) you could perhaps have two ghostly Maria Martens who come to haunt Corder and who speak their words of vengeance together. Present the three sections in order as for Act 3 scene 3.

Act 5 scene 4 – In the Street (group of three)

Tim and Anne are comic characters in the play. Tim is owed money by Corder and wants to get his money back before Corder is hanged. Two of you play Tim and Anne. The third acts as director to advise on how to make this scene amusing. Think about:

- the kinds of voices to use – what sort of accents do Tim and Anne have?
- the kinds of humour you could create with the onion in the handkerchief.

Act 5 scene 5 – At the Scaffold (group of about ten)

The play ends with a public hanging. Two of you learn your lines as Corder and Tim and rehearse a really dramatic ending. Think about the following:

- non-speaking parts needed and what they must do: Maria's ghost, the hangman, guards, clergyman and so on (maybe Maria Marten's family are watching, perhaps Corder's mother is there?)
- use of sound effects (drum beats, for example), either live or on tape
- preparing notes for the class on what you want them to do as part of the watching crowd
- decide what atmosphere you want at the end when Maria's ghost appears and Tim asks for his ninepence back – are we meant to be frightened or happy?

CORDER   Who is it?

LEE   The father of your victim, George Marten.

CORDER   I will not see him. Yet stay, [*aside*] the world would brand me coward, 15
[*aloud*] admit him.

Exit Lee

Courage, courage, William, for all your nerve is wanted now.

Enter Mister Marten

MARTEN   William, think not I come to upbraid in your last moments, though it was a cruel
act to ruin my poor child and then murder her, but now you are about to take
the long journey into the valley of death a doubt is on my mind. Tell me, tell 20
me truly, did you kill my poor child?

CORDER   No, no! I swear it. I am innocent, innocent.

MARTEN   Then heaven have mercy on those who condemn you. But be you innocent or
guilty I came not to triumph. I pity and forgive you.

CORDER   Pity and forgiveness from you! 25

MARTEN   Yes, William, we all hope to be forgiven, so I repeat: I forgive you and may heaven
forgive you too.

CORDER   Mister Marten, your words have touched my heart. I will confess to you what I
denied to my judge. I am guilty. Yes, I did kill Maria, but I have known no rest
from that moment. I have suffered a thousand years of agony. Nightly the 30
murdered spirit of Maria appears before me calling down heaven's justice. Now,
as I slept, she came to me, not as I last saw her in death at my feet but in all her
radiant beauty. It was our marriage day. The bells rang out. We entered the Church
and the words of the good priest were spoken. I was about to place the ring upon
her hand when it fell from my grasp upon the marble pavement and shattered 35
in a thousand pieces. I stooped to gather them, when the stones rolled back
amidst a crash of thunder and there below I saw horrid demons and loathsome
serpents twisting fearfully amidst burning flames. I looked at Maria. A change had
come. The fair flesh had fallen from her body and there I saw a ghastly skeleton.
Her eyes shot sparks of fire, her hands had changed to eagle's claws, and 40
seized my throat. She dragged me down, down, yelling 'Welcome, murderer,
to thy future home!' Oh, torture horrible!

When Murder stains a soul with fearful dye,
Then blood for blood is nature's dreadful cry.

He drops into a chair

MARTEN   William, William, I would not have your conscience for all the gold the world 45
could give. Repent, repent, ere it be too late! Farewell, William, and heaven
have mercy on your soul! Oh, my poor child!

CORDER   Farewell, bless you for your forgiveness. Still from the scaffold I will proclaim –
[*the Ghost of Maria appears*] Guilty!!!!

He falls in a dead faint

---

18 upbraid   criticise or condemn

4 Design a computer game called 'The Red Barn' (in pairs)

There is plenty of action in this play: ghosts and visions, gypsy characters out for revenge, attempted robberies, circus freaks, murders, runaways, police hunts, executions. Today, the events in the play could easily be made into a computer game melodrama, with Maria making her way through a series of villainous traps and dangers devised by Corder.

Work on an idea that you could submit to a computer firm. Your proposal will need to include the following:

- A business letter introducing yourself and outlining your game. You could mention the main points of the story, sound effects and music. Say how the game will provide fun, education and excitement.
- A storyboard showing examples of what the game will look like on the screen.

5 Be a journalist on *The Times* newspaper for 1828 (individual or small groups)

The real William Corder murdered Maria Marten on the 18th May 1827 (see page 68). He was tried and hanged for his crime in 1828 and the rope with which he was hanged sold for £1 an inch! Copies of *The Times* newspaper of the time show that the trial and execution were big news. The paper gave six columns (a quarter of its leading page space) to the story.

Imagine that the murder has recently been committed. Design and write the front page of today's *Times* newspaper. Study the information on this page and on page 68, together with details from the play extracts you have read.

THE TIMES

Monday August 17th 1998   **35p**

MARIA MARTEN MURDER: GUILTY VERDICT

Yesterday at the Old Bailey, William Corder was found guilty of the murder of Maria Marten. In pronouncing sentence of death by hanging, the judge said that this was one of the most cold-blooded of crimes he had ever encountered...

CORDER CLAIMS HE IS INNOCENT
Under cross examination, Corder claimed that he was innocent of the killing of Maria Marten. He admitted that he had met Maria at the Red Barn but that she had shot herself. He had then panicked and buried the body.

Parents of Maria Marten make a statement

LATEST NEWS: GAOLER SAYS CORDER CLAIMS HE WAS VISITED BY GHOST OF MARIA.

The story continues: *Many people have come to town to see the public hanging of William Corder for the murder of Maria Marten. Among them are Maria's sister, Anne, and Tim Bobbin. Tim has been trying to find William Corder because he still owes Tim ninepence as payment for the loan of the pickaxe and spade that Corder used to dig Maria's grave.*

Act 5 scene 4   A street

Enter Anne and Tim crying

ANNE	Tim, Tim, isn't it dreadful!
TIM	Eas, it's awful. I cried all the water out of my eyes. Lend us that onion I seed thee with.
ANNE	What onion, Tim?
TIM	The one I saw you putting in your handkerchief to make you cry with.

5

ANNE	Get on thee fule, I can cry enough wi'out onions. I've cried so much till if I go on much more, I'll cry myself away.
TIM	So here we are at Bury St Edmunds come to see William Corder hung.
ANNE	Shouldn't I like to pull his legs for killing our Maria and stopping us getting married.

10

TIM	Eas, and so would I, for he owes I ninepence. Dang me if I won't stop the execution and try and get my ninepence. Come on or we shall be late to see the fun of William being hung.
ANNE	Fun, how can you say so, Tim!
TIM	Well, I want my ninepence and dang me if I won't have it. Come on, Nan, dang me, but I'll have my ninepence.

15

Both exit hand in hand

CURTAIN

Act 5 scene 5   The scaffold

Corder on the platform. There is a great crowd jostling at the foot of the scaffold. Corder steps forward and holds up his hand. There is silence

CORDER	Be warned ye youths who see my sad despair,
	Avoid loose women false as they are fair!
	By my example learn to shun my fate,
	How wretched is the man who's wise too late.

Tremolo fiddles. The ghost of Maria appears on the scaffold. Corder shrieks. Tim enters, pushing his way through the crowd

TIM	I want my ninepence, I want my ninepence.

5

CURTAIN

5.4:2 seed saw
5.4:6 fule fool

5.4:9   pull his legs pull on the legs of the hanged man to make sure he is dead
5.4:11, 16 dang me damn me

The Children's Favourite Villain

Mr Punch is a terrible and violent character who has been around for hundreds of years. The script printed here dates from the middle of the 19th century. The showman (or Proprietor) works his Punch puppet with his hand, has a squeaker in his mouth to create the special 'Punch-voice' and works a range of other characters on his left hand.

1 Meet Punch, Judy and friends (groups of about seven)

Take parts and read through the whole extract. Can you identify each of the puppet characters illustrated below?

2 It's the 'Over-the-Top' Show! (groups of seven)

Imagine that you are rehearsing this script for radio or television. Your aim is to present a high-speed, highly exaggerated performance of the story of Mr Punch. The show is to have the following characters:

- a loud and aggressive Mr Punch, a real trouble-maker
- Judy, his wife, who looks and sounds like a female wrestler
- the showman (proprietor) 'wiv an accent' who tries to keep order
- a self-important, pompous Beadle (an official) who tries to be posh
- a Doctor who tries, quite literally, to beat Punch at his own game
- Mr Jones, the kindly owner of Toby the dog
- the ghost, the baby and Toby the dog (one of you play all three parts).

Rehearse and show your over-the-top performance.

Punch and Judy (1854)

Music. The Proprietor plays 'Pop Goes the Weasel' or any other popular melody, as much out of tune as possible. Curtain rises

PUNCH	[*voice heard from below*] Root-to-to-to-to-too-o-o-it!
PROPRIETOR	Now, Mister Punch, I 'ope you're ready.
PUNCH	Shan't be a minute; I'm only putting on my boots.
PROPRIETOR	[*perfectly satisfied with the explanation*] Werry good, sir. [*He plays with increased vigour*]
PUNCH	[*pops up*] Root-to-to-to-to-it!
PROPRIETOR	Well, Mister Punch, 'ow de do?
PUNCH	How de do?
PROPRIETOR	[*affably*] I am pooty well, Mister Punch, I thank you.
PUNCH	Play us up a bit of a dance.
PROPRIETOR	Cert'ny, Mister Punch.

5

10

Music. Punch dances

PUNCH	Stop! Did you ever see my wife?
PROPRIETOR	[*with dignity*] I never know'd as 'ow you was married, Mister Punch.
PUNCH	Oh! I've got such a splendid wife! [*calling below*] Judy! – Judy, my darling! – Judy, my duck of several diamonds!

Enter Judy

PUNCH	[*admiring his wife*] Ain't she a beauty? There's a nose! Give us a kiss. [*They embrace fondly*] Now play up.

15

They dance. At the conclusion, Punch hits his wife on the head with his stick

PROPRIETOR	[*severely*] Mister Punch, that's very wrong.
PUNCH	Haven't I a right to do what I like with my own?
JUDY	[*taking stick from him*] Of course he has. [*Hitting Punch*] Take that!
PUNCH	Oh!
JUDY	[*hitting him again*] Oh!
PUNCH	Oh!
JUDY	[*hitting him again*] Oh!
PUNCH	[*taking stick from her and knocking her out of sight*] Oh! That was to request her to step downstairs to dress the babby. Such a beautiful babby. I'll go and fetch him.

20

25

Punch sinks and rises with Baby in his arms

PUNCH	[*sings*] 'Hush-a-bye, baby,
	And sleep while you can:
	If you live till you're older,
	You'll grow up a man.'
	Did you ever see such a beautiful child? and so good?

30

---

4 **werry** very   8 **pooty** pretty   25 **babby** baby

3 Put on a Punch and Judy Show (groups of three)

Put on your own Punch and Judy puppet show by working through the following stages.

(a) Draw sketches of each puppet. Add some notes about their personality and the kind of voice you would want them to have.

(b) Make the puppets using old mittens, fabric and other materials.

(c) Rehearse your performance with one of you playing Punch and the other two playing the other characters. Concentrate on getting the right voices.

(d) Perform the script, or a section of it, perhaps to a primary school audience.

THE CHILD	[*cries*] Mam-ma-a-a ...
PUNCH	[*thumping him with stick*] Go to sleep, you brat! [*resumes his song*] 'Hush-a-bye, baby,' –
THE CHILD	[*louder*] Mam-ma-a-a-a!
PUNCH	[*hitting harder*] Go to sleep!
THE CHILD	[*yells*] Ya-a-a-ah-ah!
PUNCH	[*hitting him*] Be quiet! Bless him, he's got his father's nose! [*The Child seizes Punch by the nose*] Murder! Let go! There, go to your mother, if you can't be good.

35

Punch throws Child out of window. Then sings, drumming his legs on the front of the stage

> 'She's all my fancy painted her, 40
> She's lovely, she's divine!'

Enter Judy, with motherly anxiety depicted on her countenance

JUDY	Where's the boy?
PUNCH	The boy?
JUDY	Yes.
PUNCH	What! Didn't you catch him?
JUDY	Catch him?
PUNCH	Yes. I threw him out of the window. I thought you might be passing.
JUDY	Oh! my poor child! Oh! my poor child!
PUNCH	Why, he was as much mine as yours.
JUDY	But you shall pay for it; I'll tear your eyes out.
PUNCH	Root-to-to-to-to-oo-it!

45

50

Kills her at a blow

PROPRIETOR	Mister Punch, you 'ave committed a barbarous and cruel murder, and you must hanswer for it to the laws of your country.

The Beadle enters, brandishing his staff of office

BEADLE	Holloa! holloa! holloa! here I am!
PUNCH	Holloa! holloa! holloa! so am I! [*hits Beadle*]
BEADLE	Do you see my staff, sir?
PUNCH	Do you feel mine? [*hits him again*]
BEADLE	[*beating time with his truncheon*] I am the Beadle, Churchwarden, Overseer, Street-keeper, Turncock, Stipendiary Magistrate, and Beadle of the parish!
PUNCH	Oh! you are the Beagle, Church-warming-pan, Street-sweeper, Turnipop, Stupendiary Magistrate, and Blackbeetle of the parish?
BEADLE	I am the Beadle.
PUNCH	And so am I!

55

60

---

53 **Beadle** a minor local official

53 **staff of office** stick carried as sign of authority

59 **Turncock** a worker for a water company

59 **Stipendiary Magistrate** a local judge

4 Is the story of Punch and Judy too violent for children? (in pairs)

Some Victorians argued that the Punch and Judy story showed scenes that were too brutal for children to watch. Do you think that it is too violent and sexist for a modern audience of children? Work in pairs to explore the arguments for and against and complete a chart similar to this:

Punch is too violent for young children because ...	Punch is acceptable entertainment for children because ...
it shows unacceptable violence, like wife and baby battering	*the violence is so over-the-top that children will treat it like cartoon violence*
it is sexist because ...	

When you have completed your chart, debate the issue as a class.

5 Write a politically correct Punch and Judy story (small groups)

The term 'political correctness' was first used in America to express the idea that people should not use language or expressions that would offend particular groups of people. You should not, therefore, use language that women might find sexist, that different ethnic groups might find racist, that old people might find ageist, that very small people might find sizeist. It was suggested that the word 'women' should be spelt 'womyn' to eliminate the 'men' element!

James Finn Garner's book, *Politically Correct Bedtime Stories* retells well-known fairy stories in politically correct language. Here is part of his story of *Little Red Riding Hood*.

There once was a young person named Red Riding Hood who lived with her mother on the edge of a large wood. One day her mother asked her to take a basket of fresh fruit and mineral water to her grandmother's house – not because this was womyn's work, mind you, but because the deed was generous and helped engender a feeling of community.

On the way to Grandma's house, Red Riding Hood was accosted by a wolf, who asked her what was in her basket. She replied: 'Some healthful snacks for my grandmother, who is certainly capable of taking care of herself as a mature adult.'

The wolf said, 'You know, my dear, it isn't safe for a little girl to walk through these woods alone.'

Red Riding Hood said, 'I find your sexist remark offensive in the extreme, but I will ignore it because of your traditional status as an outcast from society ...'

Work in your group to write a politically correct version of the story of Punch and Judy. You will have to change Punch's name because 'punch' is too violent a word! Here is how one student started:

In an unfortunate and unintentional accident, the young offspring of Judy and Tim, a mutually caring and nurturing couple, fell from a (not very high) window.

The young person's mother was worried and, although he did not show it, his highly responsible father was too ....

Talk together in your group or class about why people should or should not use politically correct language.

BEADLE	You a Beadle?	
PUNCH	Yes.	65
BEADLE	Where's your authority?	
PUNCH	There it is! [*Knocks him down*]	
BEADLE	[*rising*] Mister Punch, you are an ugly ill-bred fellow.	
PUNCH	And so are you.	
BEADLE	Take your nose out of my face, sir.	70
PUNCH	Take your face out of my nose, sir.	
BEADLE	Pooh!	
PUNCH	Pooh! [*hits him*]	
BEADLE	[*appealing to the Proprietor*] Young man, you are a witness that he has committed an aggravated assault on the majesty of the law.	75
PUNCH	Oh! he'd swear anything.	
PROPRIETOR	[*in a reconciling tone*] Don't take no notice of what he says.	
PUNCH	For he'd swear through a brick.	
BEADLE	It's a conspiracy; I can see through it.	
PROPRIETOR	Through what?	80
PUNCH	Through a brick.	
BEADLE	This mustn't go on! Mister Punch, I am under the necessity of taking you up.	
PUNCH	And I am under the necessity of knocking you down. [*Punch hits the Beadle who falls a lifeless corpse. Punch then sings in ecstasies*] Roo-to-to-to-to-it!	

Punch exults over his successful crimes in a heartless manner, by singing a fragment of a popular melody, and drumming with his heels upon the front of the stage

Mysterious music plays, announcing the appearance of the Gho-o-o-o-st!! who rises and places its unearthly hands upon the bodies of Punch's victims in an awful and imposing manner. The bodies rise slowly

PUNCH	[*in the same hardened manner, as yet unconscious of the approaching ghostly terrors*] 'Rum ti tum ti iddity um,	85
	Pop goes' –	
GHOST	Boo-o-o-o-oh!	
PUNCH	[*frightened*] A-a-a-a-ah! [*He kicks frantically and is supposed to turn deadly pale*]	
GHOST	Boo-o-o-o-oh!	
PUNCH	A-a-a-a-ah! [*He trembles like a leaf*]	90
GHOST	Boo-o-o-o-oh!!	

Punch faints. The Ghost and bodies disappear. Punch shivers as if he has a fever.

PUNCH	[*feebly*] I'm very ill: fetch a Doctor.

---

75 aggravated assault   physical attack   **84 exults**   rejoices

6 Twisting words and meanings (in pairs)

In lines 58–59, the self-important Beadle lists all his titles and positions. Punch then twists the Beadle's words into nonsense. When the Beadle (in line 82) says to Punch that he is going 'to take him up' (arrest him), Punch plays on the other meaning of 'take up' (i.e. raise) and tells the Beadle he is going to knock him down. And he does! Playing on the different meanings of words and phrases like this is called *punning*.

To get an idea of this word-twisting and punning language, read lines 58–84 aloud. Experiment with different voices for each character. The Beadle might be self-important, proud, angry. Punch might be sarcastic, mocking, aggressive.

Imagine that a very self-important politician comes to your school and tells you all the jobs and things he does. Copy and complete the words of the cartoon below and then draw one of your own which shows Punch twisting words and punning.

7 The Further Adventures of Mr Punch (in pairs)

Write your own Punch script. You will need stage directions and information about music and action. You could try one or more of the following:

- a continuation of the story from where this script leaves off
- a ghosts scene: some of Punch's victims return to haunt their murderer
- a modern scene: a social worker visits the house to help Punch with his problems.

Here is an example to give you an idea about layout and dialogue:

Punch throws the baby out of the window and sits down very pleased with himself

PUNCH   Root-to-to-to-to-tooo-it!!

Social worker rises with baby in her arms

SOCIAL WORKER   Mr Punch! As I was knocking on your door, this baby came flying down. Is it your baby?

PUNCH   No it's not! *[hits social worker over the head]* Root-to-to-to-tooo-it!!

SOCIAL WORKER   Violence is no way to solve your problems, Mr Punch!

PUNCH   Oh yes it is! *[hits social worker again]*

The Doctor rises

DOCTOR Somebody called for a Doctor. Why, I declare it's my old friend Punch. What's
the matter with him? [*feeling the patient's pulse*] Fourteen-fifteen-nineteen.
The man is not dead – almost, quite. Punch, are you dead?   95
PUNCH [*starting up and hitting him*] Yes. [*Punch relapses into insensibility*]
DOCTOR Mister Punch, there's no believing you; I don't believe you are dead.
PUNCH [*hitting him as before*] Yes, I am!
DOCTOR I tell you what, Punch, I must go and fetch you some physic.

Exit Doctor

PUNCH [*rising*] A pretty Doctor, to come without physic.   100

Re-enter Doctor, with cudgel. Punch faints as before

DOCTOR Now, Punch, are you dead? No reply! [*thrashing him*] Physic! physic! physic!

The mixture of beatings is repeated as before

PUNCH [*reviving under the influence of the dose*] What sort of physic do you call that, Doctor?
DOCTOR Stick-liquorice! Stick-liquorice! Stick-liquorice!

The mixture of beatings is repeated each time

PUNCH Stop, Doctor! Give me the bottle in my own hands. [*grabbing stick from him
and thrashing him with it*] Physic! Physic! Physic! [*Doctor yells*] What an idiot   105
Doctor! Doesn't like his own physic! Stick-liquorice! Stick-liquorice!
Stick-liquorice!
DOCTOR [*calling out*] Punch, pay me my fee and let me go!
PUNCH What's your fee?
DOCTOR A guinea.   110
PUNCH Give me change out of a fourpenny-bit.
DOCTOR But a guinea's worth twenty-one shillings.
PUNCH Stop! let me find my purse [*takes up stick and hits Doctor*]. One! two! three! four!
Stop! That was a bad one: I'll give you another. Four! five! six!

Hits Doctor twenty-one times. Then looks at him. The doctor is motionless

PUNCH Root-to-to-to-to-it! Settled!   115

Toby, the dog, rises barking. Punch embraces him

PUNCH There's a beautiful dog! He's so fond of me. Poor little fellow! Toby, ain't you
fond of your master? [*Toby snaps*] Oh, my nose!

---

99 physic medicine   **111 fourpenny-bit** copper coin   **112 shilling** silver coin
110 guinea gold coin

The English and the Irish

The English and the Irish have lived uneasily with each other for hundreds of years. In the 19th century the whole of Ireland was still ruled by England and many Irish people wanted independence (or Home Rule as it was then called). The terrible starvation caused by the Irish Potato Famine in 1845, which the English government did little about, left many Irish people very bitter against the English.

In this opening scene from *The Shaughraun*, Claire Ffolliott, a gentlewoman from County Sligo, meets a young English army officer, Captain Molineux.

1 Judging by appearances (groups of three)

Have you ever looked at someone, or heard them speak and made an immediate judgement about their personality, income and lifestyle? Study each of the illustrations below and then write notes about each character's job, personality, speech and position in society.

- Compare your notes with those of another group.
- Improvise a drama in which your three characters meet.

Stereotypes:

When many people have the same fixed mental picture of what certain kinds of people are like, this is called *stereotyping*. For example, the stereotypical teenager is thought to be difficult, sulky, have an untidy room, talk for hours on the telephone, and so on.

- Talk about your idea of a typical Irish man and Irish woman.
- Write your own definition of stereotyping and then write about at least three dangers or problems that can arise when you stereotype people.

The Shaughraun or *The Rascal or Trickster* by Dion Boucicault (1874)

Act 1 scene 1

The village of Suil-a-beg – the cottage of Arte O'Neal – the stage is a Yard in the rear of the cottage – the Dairy window is seen facing the audience. The ruins of Suil-a-more Castle and a bold headland jutting out into the Atlantic Ocean can be seen in the half distance. Sunset – Music. Claire Ffolliott at work at a churn trying to make the milk turn to butter

CLAIRE Phoo! How my arms ache! [*Sings*]
      Where are you going, my pretty maid?
      I'm going a-milking, sir, she said.

Enter Mrs O'Kelly from house

MRS O'KELLY Sure, miss, this is too hard work entirely for the likes of you!

CLAIRE Go on, now, Mrs O'Kelly, and mind your own business. Do you think I'm   5
not equal to making the butter?

MRS O'KELLY You have only got to look at the milk and the butter will rise. But, oh, miss!
Who's this coming up the cliff? It can't be a vision!

CLAIRE 'Tis one of the officers from Ballyragget.

MRS O'KELLY Run in quick, before he sees you, and I'll take the churn.   10

CLAIRE Not I! I'll stop where I am. If he was the Lord Lieutenant himself I'd not stir
or take a tuck out of my gown. Go tell the mistress.

MRS O'KELLY And is this the way you will receive the quality?

Exit into the house

CLAIRE [*Sings as she works*]
      Then what is your fortune, my pretty maid?
He is stopping to reconnoitre. [*Sings again*]   15
      What is your fortune, my pretty maid?
Here he comes [*Continues to sing*]
      My face is my fortune, sir, she said.
There's no lie in that, any way; and a mighty small income I've got.

Enter Molineux, looking about

MOLINEUX My good girl.   20

CLAIRE Sir to you. [*Aside*] He takes me for the dairymaid.

MOLINEUX Is this place called Swillabeg?

CLAIRE No; it is called Shoolabeg.

MOLINEUX Beg pardon; your Irish names are so unpronounceable. You see, I'm an
Englishman.   25

---

7 **rise** form
11 **Lord Lieutenant** English Governor of Ireland

13 **quality** high-class person, gentleman

2 How dramatic irony works (groups of three)

Dramatic irony is the term used to describe a situation in a play when the audience knows something that a character on stage does not know. To get an idea of how dramatic irony works, imagine that a playwright has created this opening to a play:

> *Lady Smythe is spring-cleaning her mansion. She is outside Smythe Hall with her maid beating the grubby Persian rugs. The maid goes to get the carpet-cleaner, leaving her mistress, sleeves rolled up and grubby-faced, beating the carpets.*
>
> *Along comes a young, eager film company agent who has been asked to be terribly nice to Lady Smythe because his film company want to use Smythe Hall as the location for their next multi-billion dollar movie. The agent sees the grubby woman beating the carpets and assumes she is one of the servants. She realises the agent's mistake but enjoys a joke and decides to teach him a lesson.*

What might Lady Smythe do? Change her accent? Draw the real maid into the joke? Speak secret asides to the audience? Improvise this scene and show it to the class. Talk together about the dramatic effect (the effect on the audience) of this use of dramatic irony.

3 Dramatic irony in *The Shaughraun* (groups of four)

Captain Molineux makes the mistake of assuming that Miss Claire Ffolliott is an Irish country girl. Claire seizes this opportunity to have some fun at the Englishman's expense.

Take parts as Mrs O'Kelly (the real servant), Claire, Molineux and Arte (Claire's cousin). Read aloud lines 1–67 (as far as 'spare me'), then work together to present the comedy, action and accents of this opening scene. Think about:

- how Claire changes her accent when Molineux asks about her mistress (line 30)
- how Molineux treats Claire and his shock when he realises his mistake.

CLAIRE	I remarked your misfortune. Poor creature, you couldn't help it.
MOLINEUX	I do not regard it as a misfortune.
CLAIRE	Got accustomed to it, I suppose. Were you born so?
MOLINEUX	Is your mistress at home?
CLAIRE	My mistress. Oh, 'tis Miss O'Neal you mane!
MOLINEUX	Delicious brogue – quite delicious! Will you take her my card?
CLAIRE	I'm afeard the butter will spoil if I lave it now.
MOLINEUX	What is your pretty name?
CLAIRE	Claire! What's yours?
MOLINEUX	Molineux – Captain Molineux. Now, Claire, I'll give you a crown if you will carry my name to your mistress.
CLAIRE	Will you take my place at the churn while I go?
MOLINEUX	How do you work the infernal thing? [*Crosses to her*]
CLAIRE	Take hould beside me, and I'll show you. [*He takes handle of churn beside her, they work together*] There, that's it! Beautiful! You were intended for a dairymaid!
MOLINEUX	I know a dairymaid that was intended for me.
CLAIRE	That speech only wanted a taste of the brogue to be worthy of an Irishman.
MOLINEUX	[*Kissing her*] Now I'm perfect.
CLAIRE	[*Starting away*] What are you doing?
MOLINEUX	Tasting the brogue. Stop, my dear; you forget the crown I promised you. Here it is. [*He hands her the money*] Don't hide your blushes, they become you.
CLAIRE	Never fear – I'll be even wid your honour yet. Don't let – [*Up to porch*] – the butther spoil while I'm gone. [*Going, and looking at card*] What's your name again – Mulligrubs?
MOLINEUX	No; Molineux.
CLAIRE	I ax your pardon. You see I'm Irish, and the English names are so unpronounceable.

30

35

40

45

50

She exits into house

MOLINEUX	[*Churning gravely*] She's as fresh and fragrant as one of her own pats of butter. If the mistress be as sweet as the maid, I shall not regret being stationed in this wilderness. Deuced hard work this milk pump! There is a strange refinement about that Irish girl. When I say strange, I am no judge. I have never graduated in dairymaids, but this one must be the cream to the dairy. Confound this piston-rod; I feel like a Chinese toy!

55

Enter Arte O'Neal followed by Claire

ARTE	What can he want? [*Advancing*] What is he doing?
CLAIRE	I have not the slightest idea. [*Crosses to behind*]
ARTE	Captain Molineux.
MOLINEUX	[*confused*] Oh, a thousand pardons! I was just amusing myself. I am – a – very fond of machinery, and so – [*Bows*] Miss O'Neal, I presume?
ARTE	[*introducing Claire*] My cousin, Miss Claire Ffolliott.
MOLINEUX	Miss Ffolliott! Really I took her for a – [*Aside*] Oh, lord! What have I done?

60

31, 42, 45	**brogue** Irish accent	
54	**deuced** damned	
56	**graduated in** made a study of	
57	**piston-rod** a drive rod which moves backwards and forwards	
57	**Chinese toy** mechanical toy figure that turns a handle	

Here we see Claire Ffolliott and Captain Molineux in a later scene. Study the photograph carefully and decide what you think has happened to them both since the opening of the play.

4 Design the set for the opening scene (individual or group)

Dion Boucicault wrote detailed descriptions of how the stage set and scenery should look (see page 85). Write down all the information you can gather from the stage directions and the dialogue about how this scene needs to be staged. Use your notes to:

Either: Draw a picture (with detailed labels) of the set required for this opening scene.

Or: Write the opening paragraphs of a novel set in this part of Ireland.

ARTE   [*aside*] Claire has been at some mischief here.   65

CLAIRE   [*at churn, and aside to Molineux*] Don't hide your blushes, they become you.

MOLINEUX   [*aside*] Spare me!

ARTE   I hope you come to tell me how I can be of some service to you.

MOLINEUX   I have just arrived with a detachment of our regiment at Ballyragget. The government received information that a schooner carrying a distinguished   70
Fenian hero was hovering about the coast, intending to land her passengers in this neighbourhood. So a gunboat has been sent round to these waters, and we are under orders to co-operate with her. There is no foundation for the scare – but we find ourselves quartered here without any resources.

ARTE   But I regret I cannot extend to you the hospitalities of Suil-a-beg. An unmarried   75
girl is unable to play the hostess.

CLAIRE   Even two unmarried girls couldn't play the hostess.

MOLINEUX   But you own the finest shooting in the west of Ireland. The mountains are full of grouse, and the streams about here are full of salmon!

CLAIRE   The captain would beg leave to sport over your domain – shall I spare you the   80
humiliation of confessing that you are not mistress in your own house, much less lady of the manor. Do you see that ruin yonder? It was the home of my forefathers when they kept open house for the friend – the poor – or the stranger. The mortgagee has put up a gate now, so visitors pay sixpence a head to admire the place, and their guide points across to this cabin where the remains of   85
the ould family, two lonely girls, live.

MOLINEUX   You have to suffer bitterly indeed for ages of family imprudence, and the Irish extravagance of your ancestors.

ARTE   Yes, sir, the extravagance of their love for their country, and the imprudence of their fidelity to their faith!   90

MOLINEUX   But surely you cannot be without some relatives!

CLAIRE   I have a brother – the heir to this estate.

MOLINEUX   Is he abroad?

CLAIRE   Yes, he is a convict working out his sentence in Australia!

MOLINEUX   Oh, I beg pardon. I did not know. [*To Arte*] Have you any relatives?   95

ARTE   Yes, I am the affianced wife of her brother!

MOLINEUX   [*confused*] Really, ladies, I have to offer a thousand apologies.

ARTE   I do not accept one – it carries insult to the man I love.

---

70 **government**   the English government

70 **schooner**   sailing ship

71 **Fenian**   fighter for Irish independence

74 **quartered ... without any resources**   no money to stay anywhere

80 **sport over your domain**   use your lands to hunt, shoot and fish

84 **mortgagee**   one who lends money but demands you pledge your property as security

87 **imprudence**   foolishness (with money)

90 **fidelity to their faith**   keeping to their Catholic beliefs

96 **affianced wife of**   formally engaged to be married to

5 Enter the villain (groups of four)

In this play, Kinchela collaborates with the English, cheats Arte O'Neal of her inheritance and tries to kill her fiancé, Robert Ffolliott, Claire's brother. When he fails to persuade Arte to marry him, he even resorts to kidnapping to force her to do as he wishes.

Prepare a presentation of the scene from Kinchela's first words (line 106) to the end of the extract. Make Kinchela as villainous as possible. Show how much Molineux and the two women dislike him.

6 Bridget, the servant, speaks about the villain (in threes)

From the moment we first hear him, Kinchela seems an unpleasant character. Notice the way he calls for Bridget to come and take his horse (lines 108–9). Bridget does not appear – she seems to want nothing to do with him!

- Make notes on Kinchela's words and actions in this scene. For example, what plans does he have for Arte, Claire and her brother Robert (lines 112–157)?
- Two of you play the roles of Bridget and the other servant, Mrs O'Kelly. You hear Kinchela calling you to help him with his horse. Use the ideas you have collected in your notes to role-play a scene where you decide you will not go to help Kinchela. Kinchela then comes into the kitchen demanding to know why you have not gone to help him.
- Use your notes and role-play to write a drama script for an extra scene in this play, called 'The Servants', showing the evil side to Kinchela's character.

7 Claire compares Molineux and Kinchela (in pairs)

Claire Ffolliott meets two different men within a few minutes. Explore how she feels about each man by continuing this chart.

How to judge Claire's feelings	for Molineux	for Kinchela
The kind of music that is played before each man enters	Claire is singing ... (lines 14–18) This suggests ...	The music played when he appears (line 106) would be ...
What is said about each man before he speaks	Mrs O'Kelly calls him 'a vision' and 'the quality'. This suggests he is ...	He is described as 'stentorian'
What Claire says about each man	(line 103) 'That's a good fellow ...'	(lines 111–12) 'Mr Corry ...'
How Claire acts towards each man	She offers him her hand (line 140)	She does not speak a word to him. This suggests ...
What each man says to or about her and how he behaves		

MOLINEUX	At least you will allow me to regret having aroused such distressing memories?
CLAIRE	Do you think they ever sleep? 100
MOLINEUX	No! – naturally – of course not – I meant – [*Aside*] I am astray on an Irish bog here, and every step I take gets me deeper in the mire.
CLAIRE	[*aside*] How confused he is. That's a good fellow, although he is an Englishman.
ARTE	I am very sorry we have not the power to grant you a privilege which, you see, we do not enjoy. 105
KINCHELA	[*outside*] Holloo! Is there nobody at home? [*Music*]
ARTE	Here comes a gentleman who can oblige you.
KINCHELA	[*outside*] Holloo! One of you! Don't you hear me? Bridget come – come and hould my pony.
MOLINEUX	Who is this stentorian gentleman? 110
CLAIRE	Mr Corry Kinchela; one who has trimmed his fortunes with prudence, and his conscience with economy.

Enter Corry Kinchela

KINCHELA	Where the devil is everybody? Oh, there you are! I had to stable my own horse! Oh, my service to you, sir! I believe I've the honour of addressing Captain Molineux. I'm just back from Dublin, and thought I'd stop on my road to tell 115 you the court has decreed the sale of this estate, under foreclosure, and in two months you'll have to turn out.
ARTE	In two months, then, even this poor shelter will be taken from us.
KINCHELA	I'm afeard the rightful owner will want to see the worth of his money! But never fear, two handsome girls like yourselves will not be long wanting a shelter – 120 or – a welcome. Eh, captain? Oh ho! It will be pick and choose for them anywhere, I'm thinking.
MOLINEUX	[*aside*] This fellow is awfully offensive to me.
KINCHELA	I've been away for the last few weeks, so I've not been able to pay my respects to you officers, and invite you all to sport over this property. You are right 125 welcome, captain. My name is Kinchela – Mr Corry Kinchela – of Ballyragget House, where I'll be proud to see my tablecloth under your chin. I don't know why one of these girls didn't introduce me.
MOLINEUX	They paid me the compliment of presuming that I had no desire to form your acquaintance. 130
KINCHELA	What! Do you know, sir, that you are talking to a person of position and character?

101	**bog** marsh, swamp	111–112	**trimmed his ... economy** changed his loyalties and beliefs whenever it helped to make him rich	120	**wanting a shelter** without anywhere to live
102	**mire** mud			129–130	**to form your acquaintance** to meet you
110	**stentorian** very loud-voiced	116	**decreed** decided		
		116	**foreclosure** legal seizing of property		

8 Villains in melodrama (in pairs)

If you have already read *Maria Marten* and *Punch and Judy* (pages 69 and 77), you will now have met three 19th-century villains of melodrama. Below is an artist's impression of the villain, Kinchela, with some of his villainous qualities written around him.

Enjoys delivering bad news. We see this in lines 115–117 when . . .

His manner towards women is offensive. We see this in lines . . .

Complete one of the following activities.

- (a) Copy and complete this 'Victorian Villain' chart for Kinchella.
- (b) Make drawings + villainous qualities charts of the other two villains, Corder and Punch. Then write an essay comparing and contrasting all three.

9 The nature of melodrama (in pairs)

On page 68 there is a spider diagram which shows some of the typical features of melodrama. Make a copy of that diagram and add examples from each of the plays you have read from this anthology (particularly *Maria Marten* and *Punch and Judy*, but other plays may also be suitable).

- *Either* use your spider diagram to help you write an essay on 'Typical features of melodrama in the pre-20th-century plays I have read'.
- *or* write your own melodrama – it might be about a villainous landlord, a woman deserted by her lover, a bully, or even a murderer.

MOLINEUX	I don't care a straw for your position, and I don't like your character [*Back turned to Kinchela*]
KINCHELA	Do you mean to insult me, sir?
MOLINEUX	I am incapable of it.
KINCHELA	Ah!
MOLINEUX	In the presence of ladies; but I believe I should be entitled to do so, for you insulted them in mine. [*Turning to Claire*] I ask your pardon for the liberty I took with you when I presented myself.
CLAIRE	[*offering her hand*] The liberty you took with him when he presented himself clears the account.
KINCHELA	We'll meet again, sir.
MOLINEUX	I hope not. Good evening. [*To Arte, shaking hands*]
ARTE	I would delay you, captain; but you have a long way across the mountain, and the darkness is falling; the road is treacherous.

Molineux goes up to Claire, shakes hands with her again, and exits

KINCHELA	The devil guide him to pass the night in a bog-hole up to his neck. Listen hither, you, too. [*Crosses to Claire*] Sure, I don't want to be too hard upon you. To be sure the sale of this place will never cover my mortgage on it; it will come to me every acre of it. [*Turns to Arte*] Bedad, the law ought to throw your own sweet self in as a makeweight to square my account. [*She turns away; he turns to Claire*] See now, there's your brother, Robert Ffolliott, going to rot over there in Australia, and here in a few weeks you both will be without a roof over your heads. Now, isn't it a cruel thing entirely to let this go now when, if that girl would only say the word, I'd make her Mrs Kinchela. [*Claire gets to porch*] And I've got a hoult of the ear of our county member; shure he'll get Robert the run of the country – as free as a fish in a pond he'll be over there. And, stop now – [*To Arte*] – you shall send him a £1,000 that I'll give you on your wedding day.
ARTE	I'd rather starve with Robert Ffolliott in a jail than own the county of Sligo if I'd to carry you as a mortgage on it.

135
140
145
150
155

148, 159 **mortgage** money lent on condition you sign over your property as security

149 **Bedad** By God

150 **makeweight** something added to make up the full amount

155 **I've got a hoult of the ear of** I have some influence with

155 **county member** Member of Parliament for the county

The Hero with the Nose

Cyrano de Bergerac was a 17th-century Frenchman. He was a military man and an expert swordsman, but gave up army life after being twice wounded. He was said to be very sensitive about his huge nose and fought many duels over real or imagined insults to his appearance. In 1897, Edmond Rostand wrote a play about him and his love for the beautiful Roxanne. In this extract, we see how Cyrano dealt with people who stared at, or ridiculed, his large nose.

1 Don't look at his nose! (large group or whole class)

Everyone in Paris tries very hard to avoid even glancing at Cyrano's nose. One unfortunate citizen makes the mistake of looking too long.

Two of you take the speaking roles of the frightened citizen and Cyrano de Bergerac. Rehearse a presentation of lines 1–24. The rest of the group are interested observers who watch and respond to the confrontation.

- Make the opening of your presentation dramatic. Start with a general noise and bustle which changes to an expectant silence when Cyrano challenges the citizen.
- Some of you are aristocrats who hate Cyrano because of his middle-class origins. You applaud the citizen, make hostile comments about Cyrano being a 'braggart' (boaster) and show your disgust when the citizen is kicked up the backside.
- Some of you are the friends and family of the citizen. You may want to help, but you are too frightened to do much. The citizen's son, however, is rather pleased that his father has been publicly humiliated.
- Some of you are friends of Cyrano who support and cheer him. You echo loudly some of the insults he hurls at the citizen and join in bundling him off the stage.

2 Rhymes and couplets (in pairs)

Although the characters in this play seem to speak to each other quite naturally, Rostand wrote his original French script in rhymed verse and Anthony Burgess has imitated this style in his English translation.

- Take a part each and read lines 1–10. Each character often speaks just part of a verse line and some pairs of lines rhyme together ('not at all / ... It's small'). Pairs of rhyming lines like this are called *couplets*.
- Lines 11–24 have a much more complicated rhyme pattern. This is how you can work out what it is. Label line 11 'a' and any other line which rhymes with it label 'a' also. Then label line 12 'b' plus any later line which rhymes with it, and so on. Write out the rhyme scheme (pattern) like this: *a b c b a* ... Is there any line in this section that does not rhyme with any other line?
- Talk about the effects these rhymes could have on the audience.

Cyrano de Bergerac by Edmond Rostand: translated from the French by Anthony Burgess (1897)

Act 1   The Hall of the Hotel de Bourgogne

CYRANO Tell me why you're looking at my nose.

There is now a terrible expectant silence

CITIZEN Really, I –

CYRANO   Unusual, is it? Come on, talk,
Talker, tell me all about it.

CITIZEN   Really, I
Try not to look at your nose, sir, really –

CYRANO   Why?
Does it disgust you?

CITIZEN   No, no, not at all.   **5**

CYRANO Too lurid, is it? Oversized?

CITIZEN   It's small,
Beautifully small. It's minute – minuscule.

CYRANO Compound your insolence with ridicule,
Would you? My nose is small, eh, *small*?

CITIZEN   Oh God –

CYRANO My nose, sir, is enormous. Ignorant clod,   **10**
Cretinous moron, a man ought to be proud,
Yes, proud, of having so proud an appendix
Of flesh and bone to crown his countenance,
Provided a great nose may be an index
Of a great soul – affable, kind, endowed   **15**
With wit and liberality and courage
And courtesy – like mine, you rat-brained dunce,
And not like yours, a cup of rancid porridge.
As for your wretched mug – all that it shows
Is lack of fire, spunk, spark, of genius, pride,   **20**
Lack of the lyrical and picturesque,
Of moral probity – in brief, of nose.
To fist such nothingness would be grotesque,
So take a boot instead on your backside.

He kicks him. Whimpering, the Citizen leaves, his Son, not too displeased, after him. The aristocrats react unfavourably.

---

7 **minuscule**   very small
8 **Compound your insolence with ridicule**   add jeering to your rudeness

11 **cretinous**   very stupid
14 **Provided**   to be born with
15 **affable**   friendly

16 **liberality**   generosity
22 **moral probity**   high moral standards

3 Cyrano turns the tables on the aristocrats (group of about eight)

Cyrano is hated by noblemen like De Guiche and Valvert because they think he is 'plebeian' (common). They try to provoke Cyrano by making rude comments. He could easily challenge them to a duel, but he has many strategies for dealing with hurtful comments. This time he exposes Valvert's lack of intelligence by telling him all the 'nose jokes' he could have made if only he had the brains.

Rehearse and present lines 25–52. Show how Cyrano silences the noblemen's mockery with his quick wit. Remember that he is pretending to be different kinds of people who insult his nose in different ways. At line 52 finish with a *tableau* (frozen moment) showing the feelings of Cyrano and the aristocrats.

Make your noblemen as proud and offensive as you can by:
- echoing Valvert's words and improvising insulting comments of your own about Cyrano
- cheering Valvert on and giving him moral support.

4 Twenty nose jokes (in pairs)

There are several film versions of the story of Cyrano de Bergerac, including the American film *Roxanne*. This film is set in the present day and stars Steve Martin as a large-nosed chief fireman. One of the comic highlights is when Steve Martin improvises 'the twenty best nose jokes', using many different tones of voice to suit the teller of each joke.

- Read aloud all the nose jokes that Cyrano makes in lines 34–76, changing speaker at each new joke.
- Choose one or two of your favourite nose jokes. Learn the lines and rehearse them with appropriate miming and tone of voice.
- Each pair shows their versions around the class.

'They'll have a miniature umbrella made
To keep the rain off or for summer shade.'

DE GUICHE	He's a bit of a bore.	
VALVERT	A braggart.	
DE GUICHE	Who shall it be, My lords?	25
VALVERT	[*standing up*] In very bad taste. Only a pig	
	Of a plebeian would sprout a snout like that.	
DE GUICHE	So may we	
	Leave it to you?	
VALVERT	Yes, you can leave it to me.	

So saying, Valvert approaches Cyrano with a sneer of great insolence

	That thing of yours is big, what? Very big.	
CYRANO	[*Most affably*]	
	Precisely what I was saying.	
VALVERT	Ha!	
CYRANO	Nothing more?	30

Just a fatuous smirk? Oh, come, there are fifty-score
Varieties of comment you could find
If you possessed a modicum of mind.
For instance, there's the frank aggressive kind:
'If mine achieved that hypertrophic state,   35
I'd call a surgeon in to amputate.'
The friendly: 'It must dip into your cup.
You need a nasal crane to hoist it up.'
The pure descriptive: 'From its size and shape,
I'd say it was a rock, a bluff, a cape –   40
No, a peninsula – how picturesque!'
The curious: 'What's that? A writing desk?'
The gracious: 'Are you fond of birds? How sweet –
A Gothic perch to rest their tiny feet.'
The truculent: 'You a smoker? I suppose   45
The fumes must gush out fiercely from that nose
And people think a chimney is on fire.'
Considerate: 'It will drag you in the mire
Head first, the weight that's concentrated there.
Walk carefully.' The tender-hearted swear   50
They'll have a miniature umbrella made
To keep the rain off; or for summer shade.
Then comes the pedant: 'Let me see it, please.
That mythic beast of Aristophanes,
The hippocampocamelelephunt,   55
Had flesh and bone like that stuck up in front.'

---

25 **braggart**   boaster
27 **plebeian**   common, not noble
31 **fatuous**   stupid, silly
33 **modicum**   small amount
35 **hypertrophic**   hugely enlarged

40 **bluff**   cliff jutting out into the sea
44 **Gothic**   in the style of a medieval church
45 **truculent**   rude and aggressive

53 **pedant**   like a fussy schoolmaster
54 **mythic**   legendary
54 **Aristophanes**   an ancient Greek writer

5 Write a guide on 'How to deal with bullies' (in pairs or small group)

Cyrano spends much of his time dealing with hurtful comments and has worked out ways of dealing with those who bully and criticise him.

Imagine that Cyrano decides to write an illustrated guide-book called *Beat Those Bullies!* What tactics would he recommend to defeat those who set out to taunt and hurt? Work together to draft this book.

- You might start by noting down your ideas for methods of dealing with bullies and comparing them with other pairs or groups.
- When you have got a good collection of ideas together, you could write them out in Cyrano-style rhyming couplets.
- Include cartoon-style pictures illustrating each idea.

6 Write your own list of insults (individual or small group)

When Valvert makes a remark about Cyrano's nose, Cyrano tells him that if he had half a brain he could think up far better insults. Then he proceeds to do just that! Use lines 31–33 to start your own poem about insults. You might:

- write about a subject other than noses (perhaps funny teeth or big ears!)
- use the same pattern as Cyrano. State the suggested tone of the insult followed by the actual words of the insult, for example:

    The friendly: 'It must dip into your cup./ You need a nasal crane to hoist it up.'

- keep the same couplet rhyme pattern.

The smart-mouth: 'Dumbo had ears just like you.
He flapped and flapped them and then he flew.'

Insolent: 'Quite a useful gadget, that.
You hold it high and then hang up your hat.'
Emphatic: 'No fierce wind from near or far,
Save the mistral, could give that nose catarrh.'   60
Impressed: 'A sign for a perfumery!'
Dramatic: 'When it bleeds, it's the Red Sea.'
Lyric: 'Ah, Triton rising from the waters,
Honking his wreathed conch at Neptune's daughters.'
Naive: 'How much to view the monument?'   65
Speculative: 'Tell me, what's the rent
For each or both of those unfurnished flats?'
Rustic: 'Nay, Jarge, that ain't no nose. Why, that's
A giant turnip or a midget marrow.
Let's dig it up and load it on the barrow.'   70
The warlike: 'Train it on the enemy!'
Practical: 'Put that in a lottery
For noses, and it's bound to win first prize.'
And finally, with tragic cries and sighs,
The language finely wrought and deeply felt: 75
'O that this too too solid nose would melt.'
That is the sort of thing you could have said
If you, Sir Moron, were a man of letters
Or had an ounce of spunk inside your head.
But you've no letters, have you, save the three   80
Required for self-description: S.O.T.
You have to leave my worsting to your betters,
Or better, who can best you, meaning me.
But be quite sure, you lesser feathered tit,
Even if you possessed the words and wit,   85
I'd never let you get away with it.

DE GUICHE   [apprehensive now]
Come away, viscount, leave him.

VALVERT   [suffocating with rage]   Arrogant, base
Nonentity, without even a pair of gloves
To his name, let alone the ribbons and the lace
And velvet that a man of breeding loves.   90

CYRANO   I'm one of those who wear their elegance
Within. To strut around and dance and prance
Got up like a dog's dinner - that's not me.
Less of a fop than you, sir, I may be,
But I'm more wholesome. I have never wandered   95
Abroad without my insults freshly laundered.

---

60 **mistral**   a strong wind
63 **Lyric**   song-like, poetic
68 **Rustic**   like a country peasant
79 **spunk**   spark, courage

81 **S.O.T.**   stupid fool
82 **my worsting**   getting the
   better of me
88 **base**   of low, common birth

94 **fop**   a man excessively
concerned about how he is
dressed, a dandy

Rich and Elegant People

Oscar Wilde's comedies, written at the end of the 19th century, were very popular with the more educated and wealthy audiences, who loved the way his men and women talked with such ease and witty elegance. Many people think *The Importance of Being Earnest* is his funniest comedy.

In this extract, Jack Worthing (known to everyone in London as Ernest) has come to visit his friend, Algernon. As he talks, Jack reveals that his name is not really Ernest – he only uses that name when he is in London. He invented an elder brother called Ernest so that, when he is bored with being in the country, he has an excuse to go to London to sort out his brother's problems. Algernon confesses that he has, likewise, invented a very sick friend, called Bunbury, to give him an excuse to turn down boring London social engagements to go to the country.

1 What's in a name? (groups of five to six)

The name Ernest is very important in this play. Gwendolen confesses (lines 79–82) that she knew she would love Jack as soon as she heard that his name was Ernest. Jack is worried that if she finds out his real name she might refuse to marry him.

Talk together about the names of the five people in this extract and predict what you think their characters will be like. Then read the extract and see if your predictions were correct. Does each character speak and behave like his or her name?

2 What, no cucumber sandwiches? (groups of five)

To please his aunt, Lady Bracknell, Algernon has ordered her favourite cucumber sandwiches. Unfortunately, without realising it, he has eaten them all himself!

- Prepare a performance of lines 1–26 in which you show the joke about Algernon accusing Lane of not providing the cucumber sandwiches that he himself has just eaten. Decide how Lane replies to the accusation. Should he look angry? Or hurt? Or lie through his teeth like his master?
- Draw a comic *caricature* (a funny exaggerated drawing) of each person in this scene. Have word and thought bubbles coming from each character. The drawing on the right will help you get started.

The Importance of Being Earnest by Oscar Wilde (1895)

Act 1

The London flat of the wealthy, young Algernon Moncrieff. Algernon and Jack Worthing are awaiting the arrival of Algernon's aunt, Lady Bracknell and her daughter, Gwendolen Fairfax. Jack and Gwendolen are in love

Enter Lane, the butler

LANE	Lady Bracknell and Miss Fairfax.	

Algernon goes forward to meet them. Enter Lady Bracknell and Gwendolen Fairfax

LADY BRACKNELL	Good afternoon, dear Algernon, I hope you are behaving very well.	
ALGERNON	I'm feeling very well, Aunt Augusta.	
L/BRACKNELL	That's not quite the same thing. In fact the two things rarely go together. [*Sees Jack Worthing and bows to him with icy coldness*]	
ALGERNON	[*to Gwendolen*] Dear me, you are smart!	5
GWENDOLEN	I am always smart! Am I not, Mr Worthing?	
JACK	You're quite perfect, Miss Fairfax.	
GWENDOLEN	Oh! I hope I am not that. It would leave no room for developments, and I intend to develop in many directions. [*Gwendolen and Jack sit down together in the corner*]	
L/BRACKNELL	I'm sorry if we are a little late, Algernon, but I was obliged to call on dear Lady Harbury. I hadn't been there since her poor husband's death. I never saw a woman so altered; she looks quite twenty years younger. And now I'll have a cup of tea, and one of those nice cucumber sandwiches you promised me.	10
ALGERNON	Certainly, Aunt Augusta. [*Goes over to the tea-table*]	
L/BRACKNELL	Won't you come and sit here, Gwendolen?	15
GWENDOLEN	Thanks, mamma, I'm quite comfortable where I am.	
ALGERNON	[*picking up empty plate in horror*] Good heavens! Lane! Why are there no cucumber sandwiches? I ordered them specially.	
LANE:	[*gravely*] There were no cucumbers in the market this morning, sir. I went down twice.	20
ALGERNON	No cucumbers!	
LANE	No, sir. Not even for ready money.	
ALGERNON	That will do, Lane, thank you.	
LANE	Thank you, sir. [*Goes out*]	
ALGERNON	I am greatly distressed, Aunt Augustus, about there being no cucumbers, not even for ready money.	25
L/BRACKNELL	It really makes no matter, Algernon. I had some crumpets with Lady Harbury, who seems to me to be living entirely for pleasure now.	
ALGERNON	I hear her hair has turned quite gold from grief.	
L/BRACKNELL	It certainly has changed its colour. From what cause I, of course, cannot say. [*Algernon crosses and hands tea*] Thank you, I've quite a treat for you tonight, Algernon. I am going to send you down with Mary Farquar. She is such a nice woman, and so attentive to her husband. It's delightful to watch them.	30

---

32 send you down with seat you next to

3 Lord and Lady Bracknell?

(a) Enter Lord Bracknell (small groups)

Although Lord Bracknell does not appear in the play, Lady Bracknell talks about him quite often. Write down all the comments she makes about him and say what each comment tells you of the way she treats him. You could use a chart like this:

What Lady Bracknell says about Lord Bracknell	What these comments suggest about the way she treats him
'Your uncle would have to dine upstairs.'	*The words 'have to' suggest she ...*

Use your chart of notes to speak in role as Lord Bracknell, commenting on your life with your wife.

(b) Present your views of Lady Bracknell (individual)

Make notes on the way Lady Bracknell behaves towards Algy, Jack and her daughter, Gwendolen. Use the notes you have collected in (a) to:

- write Lord Bracknell's secret diary, recording life with his wife, what he thinks of her and of her dinner parties
- imagine that you have been to stay at Lord and Lady Bracknell's mansion for the weekend. Write a letter to your friend describing what it was like
- write a short essay in which you give your first impressions of Lady Bracknell. Include quotations to support your comments.

4 Poor sick Bunbury! (in pairs)

Bunbury is Algernon's imaginary friend whom he uses as an excuse to get out of boring or inconvenient social engagements (in this case, dinner with his aunt).

Improvise the following 'Bunbury Scene'. One of you invites the other to go somewhere boring or embarrassing. Your partner invents an imaginary 'Bunbury' whom they have to see. You are very interested in this Bunbury character and keep asking your friend all sorts of questions about him/her.

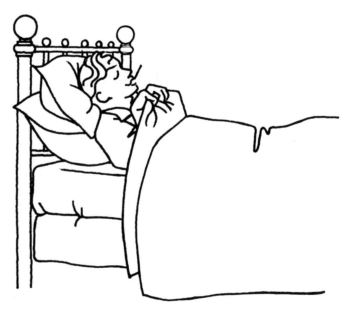

| ALGERNON | I am afraid, Aunt Augusta, I shall have to give up the pleasure of dining with you tonight after all. | 35 |

ALGERNON I am afraid, Aunt Augusta, I shall have to give up the pleasure of dining with you tonight after all. 35

L/BRACKNELL [*frowning*] I hope not, Algernon. It would put my table completely out. Your uncle would have to dine upstairs. Fortunately he is accustomed to that.

ALGERNON It is a great bore, and, I need hardly say, a terrible disappointment to me, but the fact is I have just had a telegram to say that my poor friend Bunbury is very ill again. [*Exchanges glances with Jack*] They seem to think I should be with him. 40

L/BRACKNELL It is very strange. This Mr Bunbury seems to suffer from curiously bad health.

ALGERNON Yes. Poor Bunbury is a dreadful invalid.

L/BRACKNELL Well, I must say, Algernon, that I think it is high time that Mr Bunbury made up his mind whether he was going to live or to die. Health is the primary duty of life. I am always telling that to your poor uncle, but he never seems to take much notice as far as any improvement in his ailment goes. I should be much obliged if you would ask Mr Bunbury, from me, to be kind enough not to have a relapse on Saturday, for I rely on you to arrange my music for me. It is my last reception of the season. 45

ALGERNON I'll speak to Bunbury, Aunt Augusta, if he is still conscious, and I think I can promise you he'll be all right by Saturday. Of course the music is a great difficulty. You see, if one plays good music, people don't listen, and if one plays bad music people don't talk. But I'll run over the programme I've drawn out, if you will kindly come into the next room for a moment. 50

L/BRACKNELL Thank you, Algernon. It is very thoughtful of you. [*Rising, and following Algernon*] I'm sure the programme will be delightful, after a few expurgations. French songs I cannot possibly allow. People always seem to think that they are improper, and either look shocked, which is vulgar, or laugh, which is worse. But German sounds a thoroughly respectable language, and, indeed I believe it is so. Gwendolen, you will accompany me. 55 60

GWENDOLEN Certainly, mamma.

Lady Bracknell and Algernon go into the music room. Gwendolen remains behind

JACK Charming day it has been, Miss Fairfax.

GWENDOLEN Pray don't talk to me about the weather, Mr Worthing. Whenever people talk to me about the weather, I always feel quite certain that they mean something else. And that makes me so nervous. 65

JACK I do mean something else.

GWENDOLEN I thought so. In fact I am never wrong.

JACK And I would like to be allowed to take advantage of Lady Bracknell's temporary absence ...

GWENDOLEN I would certainly advise you to do so. Mamma has a way of coming back suddenly into a room that I have often had to speak to her about. 70

---

36 **put my table ... out** spoil the balance of dinner guests
37 **accustomed to** used to
39 **Bunbury** Algernon's imaginary sick friend (see page 100)

47 **relapse** sudden worsening of health
48 **arrange my music** sort out what music is to be played

49 **the season** the social season for high society
56 **expurgations** deletions, things cut out

5 'Oh Romeo, Romeo, wherefore art thou Romeo?' (in pairs and fours)

'Wherefore' in this often quoted line means 'why'. It is what Shakespeare's Juliet says when she discovers that the man she loves bears the name of Montague (the Capulet and Montague families were sworn enemies). Why should she hate Romeo simply because he has the name of Montague? The following role-play will help you to explore the importance of people's names.

Role-play (in pairs)

One of you plays the part of an ambitious career person. You are invited to a business party where there will be some of the most powerful and titled individuals in your profession. These people could change your career for better or worse. You have to take your partner along, who happens to have a really embarrassing name. The other person plays the role of this partner. Improvise the scene where you both discuss what you are going to do about the embarrassing name.

Script work: The importance of being Ernest (in pairs)

Now see how the importance of a name is shown in Oscar Wilde's play. Gwendolen tells Jack: 'My ideal has always been to love someone of the name of Ernest.' Rehearse a presentation of lines 76–113 in which you show how passionately Gwendolen feels whenever she mentions the name of Ernest and how desperate Jack is to persuade her that other names are just as interesting.

6 Jack Worthing proposes (group of three)

Jack takes advantage of Lady Bracknell's absence to ask Gwendolen to marry him. Gwendolen's behaviour is quite unconventional and Lady Bracknell's reaction when she finds out is very predictable!

- Take a part each and read lines 104–143 up to where Gwendolen leaves the room. Make a list of the ways the two women treat Jack.
- Choose four of the most interesting or dramatic moments in lines 104–143. Present these Key Moments to the class as a sequence of *tableaux* (frozen moments) with one character speaking the appropriate key line or phrase.

Lady Bracknell: Gwendolen, the carriage!

JACK [*nervously*] Miss Fairfax, ever since I met you I have admired you more than any girl ... I have ever met since ... I met you.

GWENDOLEN Yes, I am quite well aware of the fact. And I often wish that in public you had been more demonstrative. For me you have always had an irresistible fascination. Even before I met you I was far from indifferent to you. [*Jack looks at her in amazement*] We live, as I hope you know, Mr Worthing, in an age of ideals. The fact is constantly mentioned in the more expensive monthly magazines and my ideal has always been to love someone of the name of Ernest. There is something in that name that inspires absolute confidence. The moment Algernon first mentioned to me that he had a friend called Ernest, I knew I was destined to love you.

JACK You really love me, Gwendolen?

GWENDOLEN Passionately!

JACK Darling! You don't know how happy you've made me.

GWENDOLEN My own Ernest!

JACK But you don't really mean to say that you couldn't love me if my name wasn't Ernest?

GWENDOLEN But your name is Ernest.

JACK Yes, I know it is. Personally, darling, to speak quite candidly, I don't much care about the name of Ernest ... I don't think the name suits me at all.

GWENDOLEN It suits you perfectly. It is a divine name. It has music of its own. It produces vibrations.

JACK Well, really, Gwendolen, I must say that I think that there are lots of other much nicer names. I think Jack, for instance, a charming name.

GWENDOLEN Jack? ... No, there is very little music in the name of Jack, if any at all. It does not thrill. I have known several Jacks, and they all, without exception, were more than unusually plain. Besides, Jack is a notorious domesticity for John! And I pity any woman who is married to a man called John. The only really safe name is Ernest.

JACK Gwendolen, I must get christened at once – I mean we must get married at once. There is no time to be lost.

GWENDOLEN Married, Mr Worthing?

JACK [*astounded*] Well ... surely. You know that I love you, and you led me to believe, Miss Fairfax, that you were not absolutely indifferent to me.

GWENDOLEN I adore you. But you haven't proposed to me yet. Nothing has been said at all about marriage. The subject has not even been touched on.

JACK Well ... may I propose to you now?

GWENDOLEN I think it would be an admirable opportunity. And to spare you any possible disappointment, Mr Worthing, I think it only fair to tell you quite frankly beforehand that I am fully determined to accept you.

JACK Gwendolen!

GWENDOLEN Yes, Mr Worthing, what have you got to say to me?

---

90 candidly   frankly, honestly   **98 domesticity**   familiar name

7 Witty paradoxes (individual or small groups)

A *paradox* is a statement which at first seems absurd nonsense, but when you think about it could in some strange way be true. Oscar Wilde's characters are fond of speaking amusing paradoxes. At first we think: 'That's absurd!' and then we think: 'Hang on a minute, there's some truth in that.' A good example is when Lady Bracknell first enters and greets Algy with the words, 'I hope you are behaving well', when the usual words would be, 'I hope you are feeling well.' Read lines 1–4 and explain why Lady Bracknell's remarks, although unusual, are really quite sensible.

Study the picture on the right. What word would you expect to read after the dots? What word does Lady Bracknell use? Explain what she means.

Find at least two other examples from this extract of the use of paradox (surprising or contradictory remarks) and explain how the paradox works. You could study Lady Bracknell's remarks about illness and invalids, or her comments about getting married or engaged. You could also use pictures and diagrams to help you.

"*I was obliged to call on Lady Harbury. I hadn't been there since her poor husband's death. I never saw a woman so altered; she looks quite twenty years ...*"

JACK	You know what I have got to say to you.
GWENDOLEN	Yes, but you don't say it. 115
JACK	Gwendolen, will you marry me? [*Goes on his knees*]
GWENDOLEN	Of course I will, darling. How long you have been about it! I am afraid you have had very little experience in how to propose.
JACK	My own one, I have never loved anyone in the world but you.
GWENDOLEN	Yes, but men often propose for practice. I know my brother Gerald does. 120 All my girl-friends tell me so. What wonderful blue eyes you have, Ernest! They are quite, quite blue. I hope you will always look at me just like that, especially when there are other people present.

Enter Lady Bracknell

L/BRACKNELL	Mr Worthing! Rise, sir, from this semi-recumbent posture. It is most indecorous. 125
GWENDOLEN	Mamma! [*He tries to rise; she restrains him*] I must beg you to retire. This is no place for you. Besides, Mr Worthing has not quite finished yet.
L/BRACKNELL	Finished what, may I ask?
GWENDOLEN	I am engaged to Mr Worthing, mamma. [*They rise together*]
L/BRACKNELL	Pardon me, you are not engaged to anyone. When you do become engaged 130 to some one, I, or your father, should his health permit him, will inform you of the fact. An engagement should come on a young girl as a surprise, pleasant or unpleasant, as the case may be. It is hardly a matter that she could be allowed to arrange for herself … And now I have a few questions to put to you, Mr Worthing. You, Gwendolen, will wait for me in the carriage. 135
GWENDOLEN	[*reproachfully*] Mamma!
L/BRACKNELL	In the carriage, Gwendolen! [*Gwendolen goes to the door. She and Jack blow kisses to each other behind Lady Bracknell's back. Lady Bracknell looks vaguely about as if she could not understand what the noise was. Finally turns round.*] Gwendolen, the carriage! 140
GWENDOLEN	Yes, mamma. [*Goes out, looking back at Jack*]
L/BRACKNELL	[*sitting down*] You can take a seat, Mr Worthing.

Looks in her pocket for note-book and pencil

JACK	Thank you, Lady Bracknell, I prefer standing.
L/BRACKNELL	[*pencil and note-book in hand*] I feel bound to tell you that you are not down on my list of eligible young men. However, I am quite ready to enter your name, should your answers be what a really affectionate mother requires. Do you 145 smoke?
JACK	Well, yes, I must admit I smoke.
L/BRACKNELL	I am glad to hear it. A man should always have an occupation of some kind. There are far too many idle men in London as it is. How old are you?

---

124 semi-recumbent half lying down   **125 indecorous** unsuitable   **144 eligible** suitable for marriage

8 A modern-day interrogation (in pairs)

One of you is the rich father of a modern young man. Your son has told you he wishes to marry a young girl whom you know nothing about.

Decide on the questions the father would want to ask the girl and then improvise the scene between father and prospective daughter-in-law. Remember that a modern-day young woman is unlikely to be as feeble in her answers as Jack Worthing.

9 Lady Bracknell interrogates Jack Worthing (in pairs)

Lady Bracknell will not give her consent to Gwendolen's marriage until she is satisfied that Jack Worthing is suitable. Take a part each and read lines 143–230. Then choose 5–10 questions that Lady Bracknell asks Jack and decide exactly what she is trying to find out about Jack. Record your findings on a chart like this:

Lady Bracknell's questions	What Lady Bracknell is trying to find out about Jack	Sensible or stupid question
What is your income?	To see if he is rich enough to support Gwendolen properly	sensible because ... stupid because ...

When you have completed your chart, compare your findings with those of another pair.

10 The importance of ignorance (small groups)

Few people would argue that education is not important. Yet Lady Bracknell paradoxically suggests that ignorance is more important than education (see page 106 for an explanation of *paradox*).

Read Lady Bracknell's words on education carefully (lines 155–160) and explain why she believes that a proper education is a dangerous thing.
- Why would it be dangerous for the upper classes to be effectively educated?
- Why would it be dangerous for the lower classes to be effectively educated?

11 'I have lost both my parents' (in pairs)

Lady Bracknell's amusingly absurd response to Jack's sad life story (lines 188–191) has some of the best remembered lines from this play. Memorise, rehearse and perform the lines.

JACK	Twenty-nine.	150

L/BRACKNELL A very good age to be married at. I have always been of opinion that a man who desires to get married should know either everything or nothing. Which do you know?

JACK [*after some hesitation*] I know nothing, Lady Bracknell.

L/BRACKNELL I am pleased to hear it. I do not approve of anything that tampers with 155 natural ignorance. Ignorance is like a delicate exotic fruit; touch it and the bloom is gone. The whole theory of modern education is radically unsound. Fortunately in England, at any rate, education produces no effect whatsoever. If it did, it would prove a serious danger to the upper classes, and probably lead to acts of violence in Grosvenor Square. What is your income? 160

JACK Between seven and eight thousand a year.

L/BRACKNELL [*makes a note in her book*] In land, or in investments?

JACK In investments, chiefly.

L/BRACKNELL That is satisfactory. What between the duties expected of one during one's lifetime, and the duties exacted from one after one's death, land has ceased 165 to be either a profit or a pleasure. It gives one position, and prevents one from keeping it up. That's all that can be said about land.

JACK I have a country house with some land, of course, attached to it, about fifteen hundred acres, I believe; but I don't depend on that for my real income. In fact, as far as I can make out, the poachers are the only people who make anything 170 out of it.

L/BRACKNELL A country house! How many bedrooms? Well, that point can be cleared up afterwards. You have a town house, I hope? A girl with a simple unspoilt nature, like Gwendolen, could hardly be expected to reside in the country.

JACK Well, I own a house in Belgrave Square, but it is let by the year to Lady 175 Bloxham. Of course, I can get it back whenever I like, at six months' notice.

L/BRACKNELL Lady Bloxham? I don't know her.

JACK Oh, she goes about very little. She is a lady considerably advanced in years.

L/BRACKNELL Ah, nowadays that is no guarantee of respectability of character. What number in Belgrave Square? 180

JACK 149.

L/BRACKNELL [*shaking her head*] The unfashionable side. I thought there was something. However, that could easily be altered.

JACK Do you mean the fashion, or the side?

L/BRACKNELL [*sternly*] Both, if necessary, I presume. What are your politics? 185

JACK Well, I am afraid I really have none. I am a Liberal Unionist.

L/BRACKNELL Oh, they count as Tories. They dine with us. Or come in the evening, at any rate. Now to minor matters. Are your parents living?

JACK I have lost both my parents.

L/BRACKNELL To lose one parent, Mr Worthing, may be regarded as a misfortune; to lose 190 both looks like carelessness. Who was your father? He was evidently a man of some wealth.

---

157 **radically** fundamentally
165 **duties** death duties, taxes paid when you die

186 **Liberal Unionist** a rather conservative political party of the time

187 **Tories** Conservatives

12 A haaaand-baaag? (groups of about six)

Edith Evans, who played the part of Lady Bracknell in a film version of *The Importance of Being Earnest*, really made these words her own. Prepare three different ways of delivering Lady Bracknell's famous lines (you could begin at line 201 and go up to line 211). Is Lady Bracknell angry, bewildered, stunned, amused or what?

13 The world of the Victorian upper classes (in pairs)

Oscar Wilde may have been admired by many, but he also made powerful enemies. On the opening night of *The Importance of Being Earnest* he had a violent quarrel with the Marquess of Queensberry, who accused Wilde of having a homosexual love affair with the Marquis's son, Lord Alfred Douglas. In the ensuing court case, Wilde was found guilty and sentenced to hard labour for two years for committing homosexual acts. The whole affair ruined Wilde and he was never the same again.

What picture does Wilde paint of the upper classes?

Read through the extract again and collect evidence on a chart that shows what Wilde admired, enjoyed or disliked about the upper classes.

What I think about the way Oscar Wilde presents the upper classes:		
Admirable qualities	Silly or ridiculous qualities	Unpleasant or distasteful qualities
The quick wit of characters like …	*Being concerned about small trivial things like …*	*Lies and deceit, for example when …*

Use your evidence to present your views to the rest of the class.

14 How modern are Jack, Algy, Gwendolen and Lady Bracknell? (small group)

The Importance of Being Earnest is one of the most modern plays in this anthology of pre-20th-century drama, yet even this play is more than a hundred years old.

- Make a list of the things in this scene which you think are very old-fashioned (i.e. ways of speaking, opinions, ideas, behaviour).
- Make a second list of things you think are just as true of life and people today.

Use your notes to write a short essay in which you write about how much, or how little, life has changed since the days of Oscar Wilde.

JACK   I am afraid I really don't know. The fact is, Lady Bracknell, I said I had lost my
       parents. It would be nearer the truth to say that my parents seem to have lost me ...
       I don't actually know who I am by birth. I was ... well, I was found.   195

L/BRACKNELL   Found!

JACK   The late Mr Thomas Cardew, an old gentleman of a very charitable and kindly
       disposition, found me, and gave me the name of Worthing, because he
       happened to have a first-class ticket for Worthing in his pocket at the time.
       Worthing is a place in Sussex. It is a seaside resort.   200

L/BRACKNELL   Where did this charitable gentleman who had a first-class ticket for this
       seaside resort find you?

JACK   [gravely] In a hand-bag.

L/BRACKNELL   A hand-bag?

JACK   [very seriously] Yes, Lady Bracknell. I was in a hand-bag – a somewhat large,   205
       black leather hand-bag, with handles to it – an ordinary hand-bag in fact.

L/BRACKNELL   In what locality did this Mr James, or Thomas, Cardew come across this
       ordinary hand-bag?

JACK   In the cloak-room at Victoria Station. It was given to him in mistake for his own.

L/BRACKNELL   The cloak-room at Victoria Station?   210

JACK   Yes, the Brighton line.

L/BRACKNELL   The line is immaterial. Mr Worthing, I confess I feel somewhat bewildered by
       what you have just told me. To be born, or at any rate bred, in a hand-bag,
       whether it had handles or not, seems to me to display a contempt for the
       ordinary decencies of family life that reminds one of the worst excesses of the   215
       French Revolution. And I presume you know what that unfortunate movement
       led to? As for the particular locality in which the hand-bag was found, a cloak-
       room at a railway station could hardly be regarded as an assured basis for a
       recognised position in good society.

JACK   May I ask you then what you would advise me to do? I need hardly say I would   220
       do anything in the world to ensure Gwendolen's happiness.

L/BRACKNELL   I would strongly advise you, Mr Worthing, to try and acquire some relations as
       soon as possible, and to make an effort to produce at any rate one parent, of
       either sex, before the season is quite over.

JACK   Well, I don't see how I could possibly manage to do that. I can produce the   225
       hand-bag at any moment. It is in my dressing-room at home. I really think
       that should satisfy you, Lady Bracknell.

L/BRACKNELL   Me, sir! What has it to do with me? You can hardly imagine that I and Lord
       Bracknell would dream of allowing our only daughter – a girl brought up
       with the utmost care – to marry into a cloak-room, and form an alliance with   230
       a parcel. Good morning, Mr Worthing!

Lady Bracknell sweeps out in majestic indignation

---

216   **French Revolution**   a time
      when many of the French
      nobility were guillotined

219   **recognised**   admired and
      well-respected

231   **majestic indignation**   proud,
      angry and offended

Printed in the United States
By Bookmasters